THE FAITH OF A SUBALTERN

THE FAITH OF A SUBALTERN

ESSAYS ON RELIGION AND LIFE

BY

ALEC DE CANDOLE

LIEUTENANT IN THE WILTSHIRE REGIMENT
KILLED IN ACTION, SEPTEMBER 1918

WITH A PREFACE BY

THE VERY REV. THE DEAN OF BRISTOL

CAMBRIDGE

AT THE UNIVERSITY PRESS

1919

CAMBRIDGE
UNIVERSITY PRESS

University Printing House, Cambridge CB2 8BS, United Kingdom

Cambridge University Press is part of the University of Cambridge.

It furthers the University's mission by disseminating knowledge in the pursuit of
education, learning and research at the highest international levels of excellence.

www.cambridge.org
Information on this title: www.cambridge.org/9781107432864

© Cambridge University Press 1919

First published 1919
First paperback edition 2014

A catalogue record for this publication is available from the British Library

ISBN 978-1-107-43286-4 Paperback

BIOGRAPHICAL NOTE

THE writer of these Essays was born at Cheltenham on January 26th, 1897. His first school-days were spent at St Faith's, Cambridge, with Mr R. S. Goodchild. In 1908 he went to St Andrew's, Southborough (Rev. Reginald Bull). Two years later he was elected to a Foundation scholarship at Marlborough adding to it a Senior scholarship in 1912. At his schools he showed great promise and gained many prizes. In December, 1915, he was elected to an open Classical Exhibition at Trinity College, Cambridge. In the following April he left school for the Army and after training at a Cadet School in Oxford he was appointed to a Commission in the 4th Wilts. Regiment and proceeded to France in April, 1917.

After short leave in the following September he returned to France, and was wounded on October 28th, coming back to England in November. After some months on Salisbury Plain, where in the early part of 1918 he wrote these Essays, he was attached to the Machine Gun Corps and went to Grantham in April. In July he left again for France where he was killed on the night of September 3rd, 1918.

H. L. C. DE C.

January, 1919

PREFACE

As Alec de Candole's Headmaster and friend, I have been given the privilege of writing a short preface to this little volume of Theological Essays. I strongly recommend to the attention of clergy and laity alike this young officer's vigorous profession of the faith that was in him. It is a valuable contribution to religious thought.

The boy's personality was remarkable and could not fail to impress itself on those with whom he came in contact, whether they were young or old. Of the depth in him there was no doubt from his early boyhood: the breadth of his outlook on life it was interesting to watch develop: to the height of his spiritual nature his book of poems *Avalon*[1] testifies, as well as this present volume, which he left behind him at his early death in Flanders.

When in the Sixth Form at Marlborough he was a good Classical scholar: but he was much more. He was avid of ideas and loved to wrestle with them and to argue over them. His mind was remarkably keen to detect error, and stern in rejecting it. Even more than most clever boys he was a remorseless critic, but his criticisms were

[1] This was printed privately, but is to be published in a fuller form later.

governed by a strictly logical sense and fairness. His one great object of attainment was truth, truth at all costs. It is this craving for truth that is the chief feature of the present work. The reader must remember that it is the product of only twenty-one years of life, thought and experience. But yet there is maturity in his grasp of problems and in handling them, and evidence of a deeply religious life. The author commands attention by his obvious sincerity, as well as by his ability.

Like Charles Sorley, his rather older contemporary at school, whom he greatly loved, and whom he here quotes, he was a splendid rebel: a rebel against the institutional, the conventional and the traditionally accepted, when and where, if tried by canons of truth and principle, he found them wanting. Much that Alec de Candole here writes will challenge criticism, especially in schools of thought to which he was clearly and strongly opposed. Personally I do not accept all that the boy says, but after reading his Essays I feel that he was one who had the power of envisaging truth, and truth whole. There is fresh air, and sunshine all through, and a degree of common-sense that is stimulating and refreshing. He has conviction and a trenchant power of expression. In dealing with narrowness and exclusiveness he displays a just ruthlessness, and in the face of much exaggerated institutionalism declares boldly for Christ's fundamental principles, setting Christianity before Churchmanship. Boy though he is, he expresses the views of a large number of thinking Churchmen whose opinions and convictions, I think and hope, will now gain fuller presentment after the War.

This youth would surely, had he lived, have matured into a great force. For he had the root of the matter in him. His hope for the future was ordination in the Church of England, to which he was devotedly attached, in spite of his strong dislike and vigorous criticism of certain phases and tendencies in its modern development. "The seed and full flower of all human goodness is the life and death and love of Jesus." A finer dying message no boy ever left behind him.

May this volume, with its strong and nobly expressed faith, bring comfort to that new home beneath the towers of Westminster, a home he never knew but would have passionately loved!

ST J. B. WYNNE WILLSON

THE DEANERY,
   BRISTOL,
      November 1918

CONTENTS

CHAPTER I

GOD

IF we examine the Apostles' Creed, which may be called the authoritative statement of what were in the early centuries of Christianity regarded as its fundamentals, we shall notice that it contains three great postulates, typified by the Three Persons of the Trinity: "I believe in GOD," "in Jesus Christ His only Son our Lord," "in the Holy Catholic Church"—the Christian sphere of the operation of the Spirit of GOD. In other words: (1) GOD exists, (2) His supreme revelation was in Jesus Christ, (3) He is still alive, and working: par excellence, in the society which Jesus founded—the Church, Holy because of her origin, and Catholic because of her ideal inclusiveness.

With regard to the first of these postulates, it may be said outright that the existence of GOD is not a point which can be proved to the hilt by pure reason. It is always possible, it seems to me, to believe that the world was made by chance, and acts by chance and more or less unfathomable laws. This explains a great deal; indeed, it could theoretically explain anything: for where everything happens by chance, anything at all may happen. At the same time, there is much which it does not explain satisfactorily. You may say that the sun and the stars are glowing gases: that the moon is a dead rock, shining by the sun's reflected light: that the earth and the planets revolve round the sun owing to attraction and a balance of centripetal and centrifugal forces. You may trace back the earth to a nebula and, if you like, that nebula to a part of a larger nebula, now developed and organised into the Solar System; but you have not discovered the origin of those gases, or the reason for their movement, or of their heat and their tendency to cool, contract, and harden. You may talk of attraction and gravitation, of the origin of life in a protoplasm. It may be you will yet learn to produce life from lifelessness: but what is attraction and why? Above all, what is life? What is this great principle that differentiates a protoplasm from a rock, and has developed eventually a Plato, a Caesar, a Francis? Fatalism must remain agnostic on these points. Theism has an answer, a personal Creator. Thus, at the lowest, the existence of GOD—of a personal Supreme Being—is a very sound and reasonable scientific hypothesis. And when we consider man, we are again brought up short in our Fatalism. Man is a fact, and his emotions and aspirations,—yes, his very superstitions,—are facts, whatever you think of them; and you have got to deal with them. It is no good talking about the "false fear of the gods," and saying that man's primitive belief in the supernatural is the result of his observation of phenomena—such as lightning and thunder—which he could not explain, but which are now known to have a "perfectly natural" explanation. It does not seem quite convincing to assert that men invented what they had no pattern or precedent for believing in. And apart from this, it is not only savages who have had a sincere and working belief in what they could not see around them.

Almost all the greatest men of the world have believed in some kind of GOD. Socrates and Plato were not easily hoodwinked, nor men afraid of "following whithersoever their reason might lead," yet they believed in a GOD as fervently as their fellow-countrymen, and more ideally and more rationally. Cromwell was a hard-headed and eminently "practical" man; one of our greatest generals and administrators; who started life humbly, and lived to create the Ironsides, to revolutionise cavalry warfare, to refuse a crown but rule nevertheless as an autocrat, or perhaps theocrat or conscious Vicegerent of GOD; to make England's name respected and feared wherever a hand was raised against the followers of the Reformers. Yet, though his GOD was not quite ours, we must recognise that few men have ever lived so much "as ever in his great taskmaster's eye." His sentries would notice him awake in his tent all night, studying his Bible: then in the morning he would lead his men to victory, a Psalm as a battle-cry on his lips. Belief in GOD is not the prerogative only of feeble intellects.

There is much else of what we may call circumstantial evidence that points towards theism; but there is only room for one more argument,—which may be stated shortly thus: Man is not only material, he has feelings and will. These non-material elements may even influence the physical body as when a man blenches for fear, or his heart beats wildly with excitement. Most important of all is his character and personality—quite undeniably an existent thing, which must be taken account of. Now whence is this? Can what is impersonal produce what is personal? "I worst e'en the Giver in one gift," if I wake in the Universe endowed with will and personality to find that this Universe that has made me is impersonal and unknowing. Thus it is no great assumption to say that GOD exists, and if He exists, obviously our first duty and our interest is to know what we can of Him—what His character is, and what His laws are. Then we shall know how we stand with the Universe in which we have found ourselves; and hence it is that man has for ever searched for GOD.

> ..This it is that links together as one
> The sad continual companies of men;...
> ...That souls weary and hearts afire
> Have everywhere besought him, everywhere
> Have found and found him not; and age to age,
> Though all else pass and fail, delivereth
> At least the great tradition of their God[1].

If, then, theism is established against atheism, what next? Polytheism as a recognised belief is

---

[1] F. W. H. Myers, *St John the Baptist* (*Poems*, p. 61).

dead in Western Europe at least: if we are theists, we are almost certainly monotheists. But there is a curious form of theism which has revived a little lately—the belief in a GOD Who is not omnipotent, and hence not only uses, but actually must depend on, human help. Monotheism includes dualism, if one of the two powers is definitely the stronger; but a dualism or any philosophy that leaves the Supreme Power not yet omnipotent, is a strange thing. If one GOD made the Universe, one GOD must be omnipotent in it. Or else the world must be a compromise between two or more powers agreed that a Universe must be made, but differing with regard to its nature! Whatever more GOD may be He must be at least the Sum of all human activities, ideals, and aspirations. Thus, He is supremely good. Do you demand that a man be just, pure, consistent? Then GOD must be the same, only far more truly so. Is the perfect man wise and strong and patient? So must He be to whom man looks and tends. Do men seek truth? Then GOD must be the truth—the final satisfaction of the Intellect. Are there men who seek GOD in beauty? Then GOD is there, and "thine eyes shall see the King in His beauty." He is the Righteous, the True, the Fair. Whatever is perfect is in Him; whatever seeks perfection, is from Him; whatever climbs towards perfection, is through Him. This must be so, if there is a GOD at all. This, then, is the first great postulate of the Apostles' Creed; that GOD is One, Perfect, Eternal

—the ALL. He is revealed in nature, in the faint colours of dawn, the glory of noon, the myriad hues of sunset, the terrible silence of the eternal stars. He is in the freshness of spring and the richness of autumn, in the trees and forests, rivers and peaceful valleys, barren downs and rugged mountains, in the stern cliffs and the tossing sea;

> Whose dwelling is the light of setting suns,
> And the round ocean, and the living air,
> And the blue sky, and in the mind of man[1].

He is revealed, too, in the beauty of art, in all the pictures that were ever well painted, in all great architecture and sculpture, in all music and poetry that have in any degree attained power or loveliness; no one who has ever truly known any art has not said in some sort, "GOD is here." Nor is He less revealed in all the great men who have trod this earth, in Moses and Isaiah, Plato and Aurelius, Buddha and Confucius and Mohammed, Pericles and Caesar,—yes, and Napoleon. This is not poetic fancy; no theism can say less.

But the greatest revelation of GOD that has been shown to us is not His power, or beauty, or truth, or even His goodness; but His love. We know Him now as Father, if we accept this revelation, and this was given us by Jesus of Nazareth. This, then, is our second great postulate—"I believe in Jesus Christ His only Son our Lord." We must next consider this revelation and the Person who made it.

[1] Wordsworth, *Tintern Abbey*.

CHAPTER II

JESUS OF NAZARETH

CHARLES LAMB is said once to have re-
marked: "If Shakespeare came into the
room, we should all rise and offer him a
seat; but if Jesus Christ came in, we should kneel
down and try to touch the hem of His garment."
This truly illustrates the difference between the
feelings with which the majority of us regard Jesus
and those with which we regard even the greatest
of other men. Even so wonderful and mystical a
figure as St Francis of Assisi does not affect us in
quite the same way as does the figure of Jesus.
Yet it is worth while to examine this feeling and
to try and see how far it is genuine, and how far
merely the result of twenty centuries of the worship of Jesus. For this is not irreverent, but rather
the truest reverence, to look back as closely as
possible on the real figure of the Founder of
Christianity. And one fundamental and obvious
fact often becomes clouded—that primarily, to
human knowledge, Jesus was not the Christ, but
the Nazarene—not a Divine revelation, but a man;
a man who lived in a certain country at a certain
period under certain rulers. During the reign of
Augustus, Emperor of Rome, Jesus was born in

Judaea, a country at that time[1] ruled by Herod the
Great, a monarch who had obtained his kingdom
by acute diplomacy during the wars that followed
the assassination of Julius Caesar. Jesus lived for a
little over thirty years only, and was eventually put
to death by the Roman governor, Pontius Pilate,
during the reign of Tiberius. He was thus living a
few years after the death of Horace and Maecenas,
and was more or less a contemporary of Sejanus.
This is important as we are bound in the first place
to examine His life as we would the life of any other
historical character in whom we are interested.
It is necessary, then, to find out what first-hand
evidence we have, and how far it is reliable.

Four chief works have come down to us dealing
with the life of Jesus—what we call the Four
Gospels. The Fourth of these is later than the
rest; its date and authorship are very uncertain,
and its historicity more uncertain still. We are
left with the three "Synoptists." These three
writers are not altogether independent, but two
chief sources have been traced; one lost, named
by scholars "Q," and the other probably our present "Gospel according to St Mark." This was
almost certainly written by St Mark, the friend of
St Peter, the first leader of the Church after the
death of Jesus, either at St Peter's dictation, or
else from immediate recollection of his reminis-

---

[1] Or shortly before; the exact date of the birth of Jesus
being uncertain.

cences. Moreover, as St Mark is mentioned[1] as one of the earliest Christians, it is quite likely that he himself had seen Jesus. His book is therefore our best guide. The first thing to notice in it is that Jesus is very human. He could be angry and sorry[2], disappointed[3], affectionate[4], tired[5]. But at the same time He stands head and shoulders above His surroundings. He feels Himself inspired by GOD[6] to preach and teach. He was at first popular[7], or at any rate well-known and sought after. But He came into conflict with the Pharisees, the professed religionists of Judaea[8], and at last, going to Jerusalem, He was arrested at their instigation, and the Roman governor, a weak man, was persuaded by them to crucify Him. St Mark does not spend much time on His teaching; he is more interested in the actions of Jesus; but he indicates the three main lines of His doctrine:

(1) That mutual love and forbearance are necessary between man and man[9];

(2) That religion is not formalism, or tradition, or the heritage of one nation only[10];

(3) That He was Himself "the Messiah,—the Son of the Blessed[11]": that is to say, the fulfilment of all the aspirations of Judaism, the promised Champion and Deliverer. This claim is very

[1] Acts xii. 12, 25 et al.　　[2] Mark iii. 5.
[3] Mark viii. 21, ix. 19.　　[4] Mark x. 21.
[5] Mark iv. 38.　　[6] Mark i. 15.
[7] Mark i. 28, v. 24, xii. 37.　　[8] Mark vii. 1–23.
[9] Mark x. 42, 45, xi. 25, 26.　　[10] Mark vii. 1–23, 24–30.
[11] Mark viii. 27–30, ix. 41, xiv. 61, 62.

important, for it is the final basis of the doctrine of the Divinity of Jesus. At present it is enough to say that even in St Mark's Gospel this claim is definitely and unmistakeably made. Moreover, it is plain, both from St Mark and from the other two Synoptists, that the disciples did not understand what this claim meant to Jesus. They thought He meant that He was to free Israel and rule the world[1]; they were anticipating a kingdom on earth, in which they themselves should be great[2]. This was not the ambition of Jesus as He showed in His replies to their questionings and their quarrels "who should be greatest." What the claim actually did mean to Jesus we must try to consider later.

With regard to certain other qualities, the character of Jesus has in some ways been very negligently treated. Certain marvellous and interesting points have been too much overlooked. "The meekness and gentleness of Christ" have too often overshadowed, not so much His sternness as His manliness: just as the "non-resistance" teaching of St Matthew v. has often obscured the combative qualities of Christianity, which are just as fundamental and essential, though less original. I would insist very specially on the courage of Jesus, both physical and moral. Jesus, simply as a man, is worthy of a man's admiration, worthy to be taken as a man's hero. Not only do we get such

[1] Daniel vii. 13, 14.
[2] Mark x. 35–37; Luke ix. 46; Acts i. 6.

stories as that of His behaviour to the crowd at Nazareth when He "passing through the midst of them went His way[1]"—which is less likely to be miraculous than to be simply an example of the well-proved fact that a man who shows no fear of a mob is usually safe from them: but this courage comes out especially, as might be expected, in the later events of His life. He certainly foresaw—not necessarily by any supernormal prevision—that if He went to Jerusalem He would be put to death. Yet He "steadfastly set His face[2]" to go there. And then came His arrest. He knew what would happen, that if He once fell into the hands of His enemies, they would, by fair means or by foul, get Him condemned to death. Yet through the whole scene He was absolutely calm. "Friend," He said to Judas, "wherefore art thou come?" He forbade His followers to use violence; "the Scriptures must be fulfilled." And so He gave Himself up and His disciples fled[3]. And then came the trial. "Here stand I," cried Luther to his judges, "GOD help me; I can do no other." But Jesus was even braver, for He was calmer, absolutely confident of Himself, not denying His claims, though the confession of them was the culminating evidence against Him. To all the witnesses He was silent, knowing that the evidence was false, and procured against Him by His judges. The sham could have but one issue, and He quietly

---

[1] Luke iv. 30.   [2] Luke ix. 51.
[3] Matt. xxvi. 47–56; Mark xiv. 43–52.

awaited it, with the most agonizing of deaths in front of Him. Even when He was actually on His way to Calvary and so over-wrought by His sufferings and His weariness that Simon had to be called in to carry His Cross for Him, He turned to the women who followed Him lamenting, to bid them not weep for Him but for themselves, and for their children[1]. On the Cross His first thought was for His persecutors, and His second for His fellow-sufferer[2].

His moral courage was no less remarkable. No man ever had the courage of His convictions more fully than Jesus. He found that His teaching was putting Him in opposition to the established religious authorities, yet He never wavered. If it is too much to say that He deliberately sought conflict with them, He at least never shrank from it. He did what He thought right, and taught as He believed, and if the Pharisees did not like it—well, so much the worse for the Pharisees. Whether it was a question of keeping the Sabbath, of ceremonial washings, of divorce, or anything else, if His idea of GOD opposed that of others, He met them face to face, however powerful they were. He was not afraid of Herod's threats; which indeed He treated with contempt. His call was a call to manhood; "Deny thyself," He said, "take up thy cross; put thy hand to the plough, and never look back; do not be ashamed of Me, and so

---

[1] Luke xxiii. 28.   [2] Luke xxiii. 34–43.

shalt thou be My disciple." No man can follow without courage this pattern of all courage.

Another very striking characteristic of Jesus was His absolute common sense. He could pierce in a moment to the root of things, through all the superficialities that satisfied the Pharisees and blinded the people. What do ceremonial washings matter compared with inward purity? "Ye fools, did not He that made that which is without make that which is within also[1]"? The repentant publican is better than the self-satisfied Pharisee[2]. Circumstances must be taken into account in awarding penalties[3]. You cannot possibly maintain that sin and suffering are equally awarded in this world[4]. It is important to note that Jesus recognised this fact. He was no irresponsible optimist, but He solved the problem—as it must be solved, if at all—by reference to the supramundane. His faith in GOD overcame in His mind all the difficulties of the problems of evil.

And it was the same in less speculative matters. He appreciated the cleverness of the unscrupulous steward's methods[5]. He evaded the traps laid for Him in the questions put to Him by His enemies[6]. Their own consciences must be the judges of His authority; they themselves acknowledged Caesar by their use of his coinage; the spiritual is not bound by the same ties as the material; the root of

[1] Luke xi. 38, 40.
[2] Luke xviii. 14.
[3] Luke xii. 47, 48.
[4] Luke xiii. 1–5.
[5] Luke xvi. 1, 8.
[6] Mark xi. 27, xii. 34.

all the law is love. He took large views, and it is in this matter especially that the so-called "man in the street" is valuable in his ideas on religion. The professional theologian or moralist is naturally liable to get into the condition of not being able to see the wood for the trees. The man who does not concern himself with niceties has at least the advantage of being able to see the big things.

Jesus, then, was a man—a great man, a teacher, a mystic, a hero, perhaps one whom, if any, we may call inspired and Divine—but primarily and first of all, a historical human character. His place in history can only be sketched. The early Christians worshipped Him—an important point, when all allowances are made; but in time His Divinity overshadowed His humanity, and men almost seemed to forget He was a man even according to their own Creed. Even the Reformation, though it did something by minimising sacerdotalism in the Reformed Churches, did not altogether mend matters. At length, during the nineteenth century, appeared a book which was described as "vomited from the jaws of hell," a book called *Ecce Homo*. This may perhaps be regarded at least as a useful landmark. It appealed to Christians to look at Jesus the man of Nazareth, the great Jew of the reign of Tiberius. Since when perhaps they have done so more widely and more intently. As a mere matter of historical fact, Jesus was a human being—a Jew—born nineteen hundred years ago. Any Christianity that does not start from this his-

torical fact, take full account of it, and base itself
ultimately on it, has its foundations laid on air, and
is, however good, however true even, a myth—
maybe "an ideal laid up in heaven," but an ideal
without its counterpart on earth. One result of the
prevalence of this false and unstable Christianity
has been that the word "faith" has utterly changed
its meaning. The earliest Christians meant by
"faith" a surrender of the whole being, a movement of the whole personality, to Jesus—a love of
Him, sincere and unshakeable, and a firm deter-
mination to follow His teaching, accepted by the
head as well as the heart, the reason as well as the
conscience. "Faith" has come to mean an unintelligent swallowing down of disputed dogmas—often
even of untrue and disproved dogmas, and this is
nothing less than blasphemy, a sacrilege against
GOD's gift of reason, often against the very essential Christian virtues of love and broadminded-
ness.

> Sure, he that made us with such large discourse,
> Looking before and after, gave us not
> That capability and god-like reason
> To fust in us unused[1].

This type of "faith" is what Jesus spent His
life fighting against. Ye make "the word of GOD
of none effect through your tradition[2]." "Ye have
heard that it was said by them of old time.... But
I say unto you....[3]"

[1] *Hamlet*, IV. iv. 36.   [2] Mark vii. 13.
[3] Matt. v. 21, 22, 27, 28, 31, 32, 33, 34, 38, 39, 43, 44.

"Woe unto you,...hypocrites! for ye pay tithe of mint and anise and cummin and have omitted the weightier matters of the law[1]." This formalism is one of the most unchristian vices in the whole catalogue and has probably done more harm to true Christianity than anything.

Jesus, when He died, left behind Him a band of disciples, led by eleven Apostles whom He had Himself selected. About seven weeks after the death of Jesus, on the Feast of Pentecost, they suddenly came out before the immense cosmopolitan crowd gathered in Jerusalem for the Feast, "and the same day there were added unto them about three thousand souls[2]." This was the beginning of the Church.

---

[1] Matt. xxiii. 23.   [2] Acts ii. 41.

CHAPTER III

THE CHURCH

THE history of the Church is extraordinarily interesting. The Christian Church has produced Ignatius, St Francis of Assisi, Luther, Ken, Wesley. It has produced also, or at least allowed, the Borgias, the Inquisition, the Jesuits, of whom even the worst had the official blessing of the large and influential Roman branch of the Church. The early Christians, naturally, banded themselves together, they had ties binding them to each other and to their Master which they felt to be stronger than the ties of love and kindred, and of life itself. This society, like all societies had to be organised. The only practicable method of government was that by which all religious bodies were organised; by ministers, in some way specially set apart to perform the functions of priests, to have the spiritual care of their fellow-Christians, and to officiate at their services;—by lower orders, to attend to matters of public and secular administration. The organisation was monarchical, as was all administration under the Roman Empire; and every community had its own chief priest, called the "Episcopus," that is, the Overseer—the Bishop. At first the Christians, for various reasons, were unpopular, and on several occasions they suffered official persecution. Then Constantine by his famous Edict, proclaimed tolerance and even pre-eminence, for Christianity. He enriched the Church, and was himself baptised just before his death.

> Ah, Constantine, of how much ill was cause,
> Not thy conversion, but those rich domains
> That the first wealthy pope received of thee[1]!

The Church waxed fat and prospered. That was the period of the Fathers and the "Heresies." The former were often great men, apologists, theologians, systematisers of Christian dogma and practice. But they lived in their own century, and just as they considered their own time, its ideas and its particular necessities, so must we do. In this way they have been very badly treated by some. Take, for example, the question of Fasting before Communion. It was found that some so-called "Christians" had so little sense of decency as to come to the great Sacrament immediately after an orgy of food and wine, gorged and sometimes actually drunk. To prevent this scandal, and meet this particular abuse a rule was made in many of the local Churches that those who wished to receive the Elements should be "impransi," that is to say, should not yet have dined. This wise ordinance has by some people even in the present day in the Church of England been frozen into a regulation that no communicant may taste

---

[1] Dante, *Inf.* XIX. 115, transl. by Milton.

any food or drink since the previous midnight, or
for six hours before he receives the Sacrament.
Not only does this lead to very serious practical
inconveniences (I once heard an Incumbent say
that if he cut off his evening Communion he would
excommunicate a large number of his parishioners
who could never come on Sunday mornings) but
the spirit that can lay down such a rule as a general
obligation is absolutely contrary to the spirit of
Christ and Christianity[1]. (Mark vii. 18, Matt.
xxiii. 23, Rom. xiv. 3–13, where St Paul is dealing
with exactly parallel questions.)

There are two points that this formal type of
mind forgets. One is that the Church's work is
among men. Men are individuals: every individual
is different: GOD is infinite and all-inclusive:
every individual sees GOD as it were, from a
different angle, more or less: sees more or less of
Him, more or less truly. But it is impossible to
lay down hard and fast detailed rules for every-
body, since each man must draw near to GOD as
he best can. The Church must help him; but it
must recognise that no narrow path of dogma and
tradition can be trodden by all, be it never so
ancient and never so sainted, and that some even

---

[1] I heard a story of a Chaplain to the Army in France,
who was asked by some men, the afternoon or evening
before a battle, to give them Communion, but refused on
the ground that they were not fasting; and this, when they
were going the next day into battle. One can only hope
that the story is false.

of God's truest followers may not be found visibly within its bounds at all; since though the ideal Church includes all such, the actual Church, being composed of imperfect men under imperfect rulers, is not and cannot be ideal. The Spirit of God undoubtedly works and is working in the visible Church, but imperfect man cannot become officially perfect even so. The instruments of the Spirit of God, being imperfect, cannot do perfect work; just as no human artisan can do his best work with broken or faulty tools.

This brings us to the second point that legalists forget. They are very emphatic in stating that the Holy Spirit is in the Church; but they appear to think that for all practical purposes He died several centuries ago. When one of them is asked, "What do you mean by the Catholic Church?" the answer is usually given in one form or another, "Any organised Christian body that has Bishops!" —the chief branches being the Roman, the Greek, and the Anglican. But the Greek Church separated from the Western Church in the eleventh century; the Anglican and the Roman diverged during the sixteenth. Hence the Church has said nothing with an undivided voice at least since the Reformation, and probably not since the separation of the Eastern and the Western Churches. Hence the Holy Spirit has shed no light on modern problems for four or perhaps nine centuries, and we poor Christians have to go on pouring new wine into old bottles, believing that these are the only bottles so to speak, authorised and allowed by Divine Revelation. A strange view surely!

We can now consider the "heresies." Naturally the whole body of Christians did not agree on even fairly fundamental points of Christian theology; so Councils were held, and conclusions arrived at concerning the true faith, and how far a man might depart from certain beliefs and still remain in the Church. But instead of being satisfied with defining their own position, in time the "orthodox" party began persecuting their opponents in the name of Christ.

Face loved of little children long ago,
Head hated of the priests and rulers then,
If thou see this, or hear these hounds of thine
Run ravening as the Gadarean swine,
Say, was not this thy Passion to foreknow
In death's worst hour the works of Christian men?[1]

The "Christian" Church has scarcely ever since ceased wholly from persecution, never from recrimination. For sixteen centuries the "followers" of Him Who suffered persecution and murder at the hands of the formalists has itself persecuted and murdered those who could not subscribe to their formulae. What wonder that men have arraigned the Church before the throne of Christ, or even mistakenly cursed Christ for the deeds of those who took His name upon their lips and

---

[1] Swinburne, *Tristram of Lyonesse and other poems*, p. 224.

dishonoured and denied and rejected Him in their hearts and actions?

The Holy Spirit is alive, ever working, ever energising, ever bringing forth from the treasury of God "things new and old." In the twentieth century He is with us as much as He was with the Christians of the first century, and in the same way. They applied the principles of Jesus Christ to the problems of their day; in the words that the author of the Fourth Gospel puts into the mouth of Jesus Himself, the Spirit took of what was Jesus' and showed it to His followers. And the same will be the experience of the Church now, if she will free herself from all bonds of tradition (which is not the same thing as losing her respect for the past, but is rather showing the truest respect for it in following the spirit rather than the letter of early Christian teaching and practice) and apply the principles of Jesus Christ to problems of the present day, on which the writings of the Apostles and the Fathers can have no literal bearing or authority because our particular problems had not then arisen, or at any rate not in the particular form that they hold to-day.

The Church must learn to "serve in newness of spirit, and not in the oldness of the letter[1]," to "stand fast in the liberty wherewith Christ hath made us free, and be not entangled again with the yoke of bondage[2]."

There are two chief services of the Church,

---

[1] Romans vii. 6. [2] Galatians v. 1.

"ordained by Christ Himself[1]." The first is the Sacrament of Baptism, with sprinkling of water, or immersion, and a form of words. This is the ceremony of admission, leading to many privileges and responsibilities. The other is the Sacrament of the Lord's Supper—which has probably caused more, and more bitter, controversies than any other subject in Christian history. But its exact spiritual significance cannot be defined in words, nor can a man be forced by rules to see or feel more in it than he is able to apprehend. It is primarily a commemoration of the death of Jesus instituted by Him for that purpose just before His arrest[2]. It became immediately after the great Pentecost the distinctive service of Christians. It is a service of Christian love and fellowship, a communion between the followers of Jesus Christ. It is also a service of thanksgiving to GOD for the life and death of Jesus, and of worship of GOD as revealed by Jesus. It is thus a service of communion with GOD. It has been found by many to be also an actual "channel of grace"; but this depends on certain mystical and philosophic ideas, and is moreover subjective. It cannot therefore be laid down as a dogma; though such an exceedingly widespread experience deserves the greatest respect and reverence, and the fault should be

[1] The question whether there are two Sacraments or seven, seems to depend on the exact definition of the word Sacrament, and therefore to be scarcely worth disputing.

[2] Mark xiv. 23, 24.

looked for rather in those who cannot, than in those who can, accept and realise this. Nevertheless, GOD speaks in many ways, and to many in unwonted ways.

The Church, then, is the "blessed company of all faithful people": in other words, the body consisting (ideally) of all who accept Jesus' revelation of GOD, and try to follow the principles of His teaching. It is essentially spiritual, not material. Organisation is secondary, even doctrine is secondary, to its spiritual purpose, its soul.

CHAPTER IV

DOGMA, ORDER, AND CHRISTIAN CHARITY

IF, then, this is so, what of Faith and Order—the two chief components of the Church's life, if we are to believe some? But if the Church is primarily spiritual, what are "Churchmen" to think of those whose intellectual position and religious organisation differs from theirs?

The word dogma (δόγμα, τὸ δεδογμένον, from δοκῶ), means "that which has been decided" or "seemed good"—the word used in the original (e.g. St Luke i. 3, Acts xv. 25, 28). From this third passage we see that the leaders of the early Church regarded their "dogmas, edicts or decisions"—as directly influenced by the Holy Spirit. "It seemed good to the Holy Ghost and to us," though, as we have seen the Holy Ghost works through imperfect human instruments, and the correctness of what is decided must depend on the efficiency of the instrument. The Spirit of GOD is better revealed through a St Paul than through a Tertullian, He can work better through a Luther than through a Henry VIII. So much is obvious. But it must never be forgotten that He works through all who seek GOD, if haply they may feel

after Him and find Him. All such have a revelation of GOD given to them, more or less clear and
more or less true. The highest revelations are of
the greatest benefit to mankind; but no man can
sincerely believe that which is revealed to another,
except in so far as he can himself apprehend it.
A St Francis or a Luther may bring thousands
nearer to the truth, but it is not by external im-
position, but by influence upon their wills and
spiritual understanding.

"Dogmas," therefore, in the sense of ascer-
tained and embodied truths, are in themselves
merely formulae, which themselves require individual apprehension. For example, take the
phrase in the Apostles' Creed, "I believe in...
the resurrection of the body." One man may
believe this literally: another may believe it, and
honestly say that he believes it, but in the sense of
mere continuance of personality beyond the grave:
a third may hold the same opinion, and yet deny
the phrase, thinking that it must be meant, if
meant at all, more literally than that. Most of
such quarrels are ultimately disputes, not about
ideas, but about words, the expression of ideas.
And even when the point at issue is something
more than this, when there is really a question between two opinions, it seems difficult to understand why such a difference should be regarded so
seriously, and why a "heretic" or "unorthodox"
person should be treated so severely. It is as hard
to accept a dogma as to do right—a point well

worked out in *Ecce Homo*[1]. Most men are comparatively tolerant of errors in action, because they have to act themselves and so know the difficulties of right action. But a man who accepts dogmas because he never thinks—who "believes" (or says he believes) to save the trouble of thought —is usually very hard on errors of "faith"—because he does not know the difficulty of belief. Yet take a thinker versed in abstractions, with little practical experience; he will probably find "Thou shalt love thine enemy, and thy neighbour as thyself" a much less hard saying than "the Word was made flesh"—the Absolute and Infinite expressed in concrete human terms, the Eternal Spirit confined in flesh, the All born of a woman! Yet such amazing mysteries we are bidden accept, and condemned if we fail to "believe"; when we can scarcely even comprehend what it is that we are required to accept!

The notion therefore that one man, or one formula, or one Creed, or one Church, can apprehend the whole truth of GOD is palpably absurd. GOD is infinite: mankind a finite collection of finites. The utmost that any Church can claim is that it contains all that it is possible for man to know of GOD: and this is also obviously false unless that Church actually (and not merely ideally) contains every member of the human race. The lowest savage even is different from all his fellow men, with some capacity that no one else has,

[1] Part I, Chapter VII.

some special vision of GOD to communicate to the world. This is not fancy: it is pure reason: it is the sternest and the most prosaic logic—unless we are to grant the impossible idea that any two men are, have been, or ever will be, exact spiritual replicas of each other.

Or it may be said that this or that Church contains all the truth of GOD that it is right for man to know. In that case, either we have the capacity (the GOD-given capacity, since GOD made us) to know more than GOD wills or intends us to know; or else, all apprehension and reasoning outside this Church is false, which would be a very rash thing to assert. You cannot deny alleged truths in a lump, without knowing and having examined all that the lump contains: and moreover, even opinions that are superficially incompatible, are often (and perhaps always, could we probe deep enough to see it) really complementary.

GOD is too great to be comprised in any human formula, creed or Church whatsoever: those who look to find GOD's whole truth in a formula, creed or Church, are worshipping a petty Deity, contemptible even to man.

Don't nail God down to rules, and think you know!
    Or God, Who sorrows all a summer's day
Because a blade of grass has died, will come
    And suck this world up in His lips, and lo!
Will spit it out a pebble, powdered grey,
    Into the whirl of Infinity's nothingless foam[1].

[1] H. Rex Freston, *Collected Poems*, p. 112.

And the same principles must be applied to the question of Order. The worship of Order is even more absurd and unchristian than the worship of Dogma. The narrow dogmatist has at any rate this that can be said for him: that he does think that his dogmas contain the truth about GOD, and that those who do not hold his dogmas are in error about the most important matters; which is at least the result of zeal for truth, though a narrow or mistaken zeal. But the man who despises another because their religious organisation is not the same, holds a position too ridiculous to be easily combated. His argument is: organisation is necessary for any religious body: for fifteen hundred years the Christian Churches were all episcopally organised; this is obviously due to the guidance of the Spirit of GOD. Episcopacy is, therefore, GOD's will. Any sect that rejects episcopacy is no true part of the Church of Christ, and must necessarily lack the special grace of ministry in its officers, since this grace is only transmitted by bishops, the only true successors of the Apostles, to whom the grace was given from Jesus Christ Himself. Moreover, the Holy Communion may only be given to Christians who have been confirmed: confirmation is the prerogative of bishops: therefore no member of a non-episcopal Church can receive truly the Sacrament of the Body and Blood of Christ.

Now this argument first of all ties GOD down to a formula, denying that the grace of ministry can be given save through bishops. "Don't nail GOD down to rules, and think you know!" Cannot GOD give His grace as He wills, to whom He wills, how He wills? Are the fountains of this grace stopped, that we have to go back two thousand years for it? The GOD who sent His Spirit on the first Christians on that great Pentecost, can He not send down His Spirit now upon Non-conformist Ministers? The Jesus Who gave the first Sacrament to His disciples, to whom His commission even was not yet given, shall He refuse His presence to His followers at the Sacrament because, forsooth, no bishop has laid his hands upon them?

But our worshipper of Order will reply: GOD has tied Himself to these channels in His dealings with us, and we must follow His will, and use these channels and these only. I deny it. GOD never yet tied Himself to any one channel in dealing with the myriad-souled race of men. With all their fifteen hundred years of tradition, these channels are, at most, GOD's normal methods: but are we to deny GOD the right ever to depart from His normal methods? If we are to judge men, or Churches, by their fruits, shall we prefer the narrowness and heresy-hunting of our extreme Episcopalians, to the purity of the Quakers, the piety of the Wesleyans, and the freedom of the Congregational bodies? "Where two or three are gathered together in My name, there am I in the midst of them[1]," is the word of Jesus: gathered

[1] Matt. xviii. 20.

that is, in the Spirit of Jesus, in humility and fearlessness and sincerity and devotion and thankfulness and desire and love: not in strict adherence to human traditions; not with exact enquiry, "Have you been confirmed by a bishop? Do you believe this and that and the other thing?" It is this narrowness, this attitude of not being able to see the wood for the trees, this twist of soul that makes the secondary loom larger than the primary, that seems to have been the one thing capable of rousing Jesus to fury[1]. He could be exceedingly, terribly angry, enraged, furious; seldom has there been heard a more terrific and comprehensive denunciation than that contained in Matt. xxiii.: and it was directed all against this very type of mind. For however important Faith and Order may be, there is one thing greater still —the vital and fundamental principle of Christianity—charity, large mindedness, love. Are you going to condemn your Non-conformist brother —for whom Christ died—for not having bishops? Are you going to condemn your perplexed brother —for whom Christ died—for not being able to subscribe to your formulae? "Now abideth faith, hope, love, these three; but the greatest of these is love[2]."

[1] Matt. xxiii. 16–26.   [2] I Cor. xiii. 13.

CHAPTER V

INFALLIBILITY

THE search for an infallible guide in matters of religious truth is probably as old as religion itself. To this extent it is good—that it is the result of the realisation that on any subject a man versed in that subject should be listened to with attention and respect. But when this mere platitude stiffens into an assertion that any man whatever, however wise, is always and unquestionably right on any subject, then we have the beginning of the terrible impiety of intellectual slavery. Some men, it is said, are born slaves: they cannot work save under the eye of a master, and a master of some sort they will find for themselves. This is certainly true intellectually: a very large number of men lack either the energy, or the ability, or both, to think for themselves. Hence they seek an infallible Church, an infallible Book, or an infallible authority of some kind, and therein they find "peace"—the peace of the man who has refused the fight.

Now this may perhaps be defensible for the individual: but the point is always carried further, and those who still maintain their intellectual freedom, are denounced, are bidden surrender it, and invited to enslave themselves in "peace," like their fellows. This demand is both unreasonable and impious. Unreasonable, because reason demands its freedom: impious, because this reason that demands freedom is from GOD. It is useless to argue that reason may be used within the limits allowed by dogma: for that argument, in plain terms, runs thus: You may use your reason: if you come to my conclusion, well and good: if you do not, then you must deny the result of your reasoning. If a definite conclusion must be arrived at, you had better accept it straight away; to bolster up by argument a foregone result is intellectual and spiritual dishonesty. Moreover, as has already been pointed out, you cannot comprise GOD in a formula; and in any case, a formula is only an expression, needing further definition, and only capable of unexpressed, but felt, definition in the individual mind and soul.

The two chief sources to which Christians have looked for infallible guidance are the Church and the Bible. The theory of verbal inspiration is, I hope and believe, dying. It is too obviously absurd to last much longer in the light of examination. The very arithmetical discrepancies of the Bible give away the principle, and most striking of all it does not seem to have been noticed by those who hold this view that Jesus Himself laid down the principle in the light of which Christians should study the Old Testament. In the Sermon on the Mount, He claims to have come to "fulfil the law," and He proceeds to give several concrete instances of this "fulfilment," with regard to murder and hatred, adultery and lust, the questions of divorce, swearing, revenge, and the treatment of enemies[1]. He announced the principle of development, or progressive revelation. The "righteousness of the Scribes and Pharisees" which He commanded His followers to exceed[2], was just this formal legalist spirit that believes in and holds to, one fixed moral or theological code, a faith once for all delivered, and thenceforward unchangeable. The Old Testament, Jesus said, is imperfect; He came to fulfil it. And He did fulfil it, to the extent that He laid down what is yet the final word in human ethics and morality: "Thou shalt love."

But human knowledge and human thought have gone forward in the last nineteen hundred years; and just as Jesus never pretended to teach science, so He never claimed to teach theology. His mission was entirely practical, though His revelation of GOD as a loving Father has revolutionised theology. He never laid down a Creed. It is worth while noting that Jesus never condemned anyone for intellectual perplexity or even error. The people whom He did condemn were the earthly minded[3], the censorious[4], the hypocrites[5],

[1] Matt. v. 21–48.
[2] Matt. v. 20.
[3] Mark x. 23–25; Luke xii. 13–21.
[4] Matt. vii. 3–5, ix. 10–13, xi. 16, 19.
[5] Matt. vii. 21–23.

those who persisted in wilful blindness to good[1], the formalists[2], the uncharitable or revengeful[3].

On the other hand, the story told us by the author of the Fourth Gospel (a mystic and not apparently a man with a great deal of sympathy for intellectual perplexity) regarding St Thomas' doubt of Jesus' resurrection[4], is remarkably instructive. The disciples were convinced that Jesus had risen from the dead—a most amazing event; we are apt to forget how amazing. But they were persuaded that Jesus had appeared to them. (We are now dealing with the story as told us; the author had no doubt of the reality of the Resurrection, therefore the story can be accepted as illustrating the attitude of Jesus towards intellectual perplexity, even by those who do not believe in the Resurrection; and all the more so because of the comparative narrowness of the narrator himself.)

Thomas, however, had not been with them, and could not believe this astounding statement, and like an honest man said so, reserving his judgment for further evidence. Now our "orthodox" Christians (who have always been hardly inclined even towards St Thomas) would have persecuted him —"you *shall* believe! Your doubts are devil-born. Put them away." Not so Jesus. "After eight days

[1] Mark iii. 22–30.
[2] Mark vii. 1–23, ii. 23, 28, iii. 1, 5; Matt. xvi. 1, 4, xxiii.; Luke xi. 37–52.
[3] Matt. xxv. 41, 45; Luke ix. 52, 56.
[4] John xx. 24–29.

again His disciples were within and Thomas with them; then came Jesus, the doors being shut, and stood in the midst. . . . Then saith He to Thomas, Reach hither thy finger and behold My hands; and reach hither thy hand, and thrust it into My side; and be not faithless but believing." This was the very evidence that Thomas had demanded. Jesus respected his doubts, sympathised with his perplexities, and offered him the evidence he wanted. The sentence that follows the confession of Thomas is not a condemnation of his doubts; it is simply a blessing pronounced on those who have spiritual insight. For there are human faculties that transcend reason; and blessed are they who have that spiritual insight which leads to that Christian faith already defined as a movement of the whole personality towards Jesus. But it was not Jesus, but His self-styled "followers" who have been the persecutors of intellectual error.

The belief in the infallibility of the Church is a rather curious superstition, and exceedingly vague. The man who tells us that the Bible is infallible is at least definite: he puts a certain volume into our hands; Here is a volume, he can say, consisting of sixty-six books, and divided into two Testaments. It was written by such and such people about such and such times: you can read it for yourself; this is your guide. Follow it. But the infallible Church is a Fata Morgana's palace; the more you try to follow it, the more shadowy and unattainable it grows. For what is this Church? asks the be-

wildered seeker after truth; and is told that it is
any organised Christian body that has bishops.
What, then, he asks, of others? They are not
Christian bodies, is naturally the reply, though a
little hard if said, for example, of certain Non-
conformists. And how, in any given split of
opinion between episcopal bodies, may one decide
which is the Church and which the heretical
party? "The Church is the side which is right,"
was an answer I once actually received. This,
then, is the argument: "The Church is infallibly
right; for whichever side is right is the Church!"
Which leaves the poor bewildered seeker after
Truth much where he was.

Or, again, at least three large Christian bodies
are to-day comprised, according to this definition,
in the Catholic Church—the Roman, the Greek,
and the Anglican. Now granted that they will all
repeat certain formulae: "I believe in GOD...in
Jesus Christ His only Son our Lord, Who was born
of the Virgin Mary...in the Resurrection of the
body..." and so on. But even if the further
official definition of these tenets were the same—
which I doubt—what of further and more detailed
doctrine:—of the Lord's Supper, of the grace of
Orders, of the position of Non-conformists, of
Papal predominance? The Catholic Church, even
so narrowly defined as above, speaks with no certain voice, and has, as I say, spoken with nothing
but confused voices since the Reformation, perhaps since the separation of the Eastern and

Western Churches. And our seeker after truth has no chance of finding out whether the Church is really infallible—he cannot even find the Church! The fact is, that these preachers of the infallibility of the Church live, spiritually, before the eleventh century: they have no grasp of more modern questions, in so far as they do really hold to this professed belief of theirs. And even the early Fathers, and the Apostles themselves—great and valuable as they were, and immense as is our debt to them even now—were human, and men of their age at that: so they cannot be expected to give detailed answers to modern problems.

But Jesus Christ at least, we are told, is infallible. He however, dealt with theological questions not much, with theological details not at all: with intellectual questions not at all[1]. He is, and remains, the greatest religious teacher of the world: but even He was a Jew of the first century of our era, and held (for example, on eschatological questions) the views of a Jew of the first century of our era. Or you may say that He used His contemporaries' language figuratively; which leaves us where we were; for if we cannot take His eschatological prophecies literally, where are we to stop?

Therefore we cannot accept even the detailed prophecies of Jesus as infallible; but His principles stand firm; His great and fundamental principle of love remains; His condemnation of world-

[1] See e.g. Luke xiii. 23, 24.

liness, unkindness, selfishness, hypocrisy, formalism—this is unshaken. We are not here to obey rules like children but to apply principles, to struggle, to seek, to endure, like men. We are on earth as an education—perhaps the beginning of an eternal one—and we must fight against slavishness in our education; we who are the free sons of GOD.

> I do not know if it seems brave
> The youthful spirit to enslave,
> And hedge about, lest it should grow.
> I don't know if it's better so
> In the long end. I only know
> That when I have a son of mine,
> He shan't be made to droop and pine,
> Bound down and forced by rule and rod
> To serve a God who is no God.
> But I'll put custom on the shelf
> And make him find his God himself...
>> A God—who will be all his own,
>> To whom he can address a prayer
>> And love him, for he is so fair,
>> And see with eyes that are not dim
>> And build a temple meet for him[1].

[1] C. H. Sorley, *Marlborough and other poems*, p. 10.

CHAPTER VI

REASON AND FAITH

THERE is a curious idea that there is something impious in the free use of reason in religious matters. Reason, as all would grant, I hope, is a gift of GOD; but it is, according to some, only "meant" to be used in purely earthly things—in politics, in adding up £. s. d.; in organising charity bazaars. But when you reach the highest things and the most important (and incidentally the most difficult) you must shut out reason and have "faith." In other words, you may use your rudder in calm seas; but when you enter a storm, you must dispense with it. But religion, if it is to be anything at all, must be the concern of the whole being—intellectual, moral, aesthetic. GOD is the All: He is at least the sum of all our aspirations. Do we desire Truth? GOD is the Truth, and Jesus is for Christians the supreme Revealer of Truth. Do we desire Righteousness? GOD is the supreme Righteousness, and Jesus is the Way. Do we desire Beauty? GOD is the All-Lovely, and Jesus the Life. If a politician, or man of business, or lawyer, or doctor, or soldier, is useless without reason, much more a man whose chief concern is GOD—as should be all men's. GOD is the Truth; and religion is maimed without philosophy, just as it is maimed without love of moral or aesthetic excellence. And philosophy, like all other human activities, must have free scope. If philosophy errs, it must be corrected; not simply rejected, though rejection is the simpler plan—till that which is rejected takes revenge. Does religion despise Art? Then it produces men who give Art the place of religion. Does it despise Philosophy? Then you get a Gibbon. Philosophy and Art are activities of human nature; and human nature cannot be thus summarily expelled—she will come back, with vengeance at her heels.

All this does not deny that there are spheres where reason is useless. You cannot by searching find out the Almighty to perfection; mystical knowledge transcends intellectual knowledge. But reason must be combated with reason, not with authority; for true reason recognises its own limitations. Just as true Art realises that it has no necessary place in the moral sphere, and true morality that it has no authority in the realms of beauty: so true reason knows that the infinite is beyond it. But an unintelligent faith is worse than useless—it is false. You may not understand, but only be able to feel, your belief: but you must at least understand what it is that you believe. Take an example: "I believe that Jesus is the Son of GOD." You may believe that, yet not be able to reason out how He is the Son of GOD; but you must have a definite feeling about the meaning of the matter. You may mean one thing by it;

another may mean a different thing by the same phrase. If some one bids you believe that Jesus is the Son of GOD, you have a right to ask him what he means by the phrase. You may say, " I don't understand what you mean when you say this." If he answers, "You cannot understand it, it is a mystery: all you have to do, is to believe it," his words may be unimpeachable, but his meaning is ridiculous. When I say that I believe the earth is round, I may not be able to prove it: if a person doubted it I might have to send him on elsewhere, or I might—if I was very ignorant or obstinate— refuse to believe it at all; but at least I do know what a person means when he says that the earth is round. He means that this mass of matter on which we live is on the whole of a certain definite shape, which we call round or spherical. Now we have something to start from. But does "Jesus is the Son of GOD" mean that He is the same as the Eternal Ruler of all things, or like Him, or inspired by Him, or merely divine in the sense in which all men are divine—the Son of GOD in the sense in which all men are sons of GOD? Define thus far, and we have something to start from. If he says that Jesus is like GOD—the same as GOD, but human as well, we still have a right to ask to be given at least a general idea of what this means. You cannot believe a thing unless you at least understand the expression of your faith. Otherwise your Creed becomes so much Chinese.

Or take another example. You may say that

"man is very far gone from original righteousness,
and is of his own nature inclined to evil...and
therefore in every person born into this world it
[that is, original sin] deserveth GOD'S wrath and
damnation[1]." Now reason, and man's moral conscience (which, when free and unvitiated is
usually the ally of reason) might pause over this
last sentence and ask: How can a baby at its birth
deserve GOD'S wrath and damnation? The moral
conscience asserts that this is unjust: reason adds,
that if GOD be GOD, He is just, and even if human
nature is evil, the individual is not therefore
necessarily guilty—which may or may not be
sound. But it cannot be crushed by authority, or
waved aside with the remark that if so, you are in
disagreement with the Church of England. That
may be true, but is completely off the point, since
there is no law that states that the English bishops
and the clergy of 1562 were necessarily infallible.
You must meet reason with reason.

Or again, you may say that the Bible teaches the
doctrine of Eternal Punishment. I believe it is
possible to twist all the texts quoted in favour of
this doctrine so that they do not necessarily mean
that. If an objector were to take a larger view, and
say that if GOD is loving He will not do to anyone
a thing that no one would do to his worst enemy:
that if GOD is just, He will not avenge with infinite
penalties finite offences, or condemn to hopeless
torment a soul that never willed to be created:

[1] Book of Common Prayer, Article IX.

that if GOD is wise He will not inflict punishment for sheer revenge—for endless punishment can only be revengeful since it never can be remedial; —if he says this, it is no good to quote texts at him or passages from the Fathers, or decrees of the Church. If you answer him at all, you must do so by argument. You must meet reason with reason, not with authority. Authority leads to ruin: for it makes change and progress impossible. A thing may once have been true for us, but our knowledge of truth progresses. We have now seen further and higher and purer truth: and that we must follow, "forgetting those things which are behind, and reaching forward to those things which are before." And reason is one of our GOD-given faculties, to be used with all our other faculties, in the apprehending of GOD. For we cannot, without great loss, ignore or despise any of our faculties by refusing to use them in our religion. And this is true in any sphere whatever.

There are some who are inclined to despise reason, and some who are inclined to despise emotion and mysticism. But just as reason must be respected, so must these. Man is not wholly material. A man most certainly feels emotions— emotions which may even affect his body: and it is just as absurd to attempt to ignore these as it is to attempt to ignore reason. In fact, the motive power of man lies in his non-material being, his emotions, his personality, his will. It is his will that forces a man to do what is unpleasant because it is right; it is his personality that is the source of his influence on others. It was the stern will of Hannibal that shook Rome, it was the unbending will of Garibaldi that saved Italy; it was the untiring will of Wilberforce and his colleagues that abolished slavery in the British Empire. It was the personality of Caesar that led his legions to victory; it was the personality of Napoleon that so bound his soldiers to him that they conquered half Europe. Even reason cannot control the will, until the will itself decides to be governed by reason; and even then it may at any time revolt.

And the value, too, of emotion and mysticism is very great. They are undoubtedly faculties of human nature—though, like reason and all other faculties, far more highly developed in some than in others—and have done far too much to be despised without stupidity, or ignored without great loss. The study of hypnotism has added much to our knowledge of what is called our psychical power; a man's will can be temporarily put under complete subjection to the will of another; then the subject is absolutely under the control of the hypnotiser, body and mind. The subject will do whatever he is told; even blisters, of greater or less severity, may be produced on his body, at the suggestion of the hypnotiser. The will of man is the strongest power on earth. It can conquer all things, and endure all things. We cannot, then, afford to ignore our non-material and emotional powers. A certain amount of self-hypnotism there undoubtedly is and has been; but to explain all mysticism by this is not an explanation adequate to the facts.

Now there are two great points in Christianity on which mysticism has especially seized—the Divinity of Jesus and the Holy Communion. Many have spoken from personal experience of the former; of the help and presence of Jesus which they have themselves actually felt. They have told us of their own experience of the power of prayer.

Now at these problems reason confessedly fails: the intellectual difficulties of prayer, no less than of accepting the Divinity of Jesus, are enormous and almost overwhelming. But to reject for this cause the vast mass of mystical evidence on these problems is blasphemy to mankind; for you shut the door on certain human faculties, thereby excluding the light that comes through them. This evidence cannot be ignored without disaster, any more than can the evidence of reason. And it is the same with the Holy Communion; many have found in it their closest approach to GOD through Jesus and though, as we have seen, this does not justify dogmatism, it does demand most careful and sincere consideration. GOD is the Truth and must be sought by reason: but He is also a Spirit, and must be sought by the spirit of man. It takes at least the whole man to contemplate the All.

CHAPTER VII

THE MIRACULOUS ELEMENT
IN JESUS

A POINT that sticks in the throat of a good many people to-day is the alleged miraculous element in the life of Jesus: His miracles of healing, power over nature, and raising the dead; the doctrine of His Virgin Birth; and the story of His resurrection. This last is the most important, and throws light perhaps on the others. It is a most astonishing story, *a priori* extremely improbable, and therefore requiring the strongest evidence in its favour if it is to be accepted. But, I think it has this. No one ever claimed to have actually seen the event; the only people said to be present were the Roman guard, and they were asleep. But the circumstantial evidence is overwhelming. Consider at the Passover, when Jesus was arrested, His followers were a weak and timorous band, "they all forsook Him and fled[1]." Their leader plucked up courage to go as far as the palace of the high priest beneath the court of Justice; but when he was suspected of dealings with Jesus, he three times flatly and vehemently denied any such thing[2]. At most one other, the chosen and closest friend of Jesus, and some

[1] Mark xiv. 50.   [2] Mark xiv. 66–72.

women, were by His Cross, or standing afar off[1]
After the death of Jesus they met, if at all,
secretly[2]. This was at the time of the Passover.
Seven weeks later came the feast of Pentecost, and
again Jerusalem was crowded with Jews and prose-
lytes from all parts of the Mediterranean world.
Before them rose up these same once timid
followers of Jesus, led by the Peter who had three
times denied Him, and this Peter preached to
them that Jesus whom they had seen crucified at
the Passover had been raised from the dead[3].
Three thousand joined Peter[4] and the Christian
Church began. They were persecuted by the
religious authorities[5] who were however unable
to shut their mouths. Some left Jerusalem for
Samaria, Antioch, and other places: and eventually, largely through the efforts of St Paul (who
had at first been one of the most eager persecutors
of the Christians), the story spread to Europe and
in time reached Rome.

Now we have this extraordinary phenomenon;
for at least twelve hundred years Christianity was
one of the most potent factors in European politics.
This Christianity began from Judaea, from a few
uninfluential people, who by force of sheer energy

---

[1] John xix. 25, 26; Mark xv. 40, 44.
[2] John xx. 19.   [3] Acts ii. 22–24, 32, 33.
[4] Acts v. 41.
[5] Acts iv. 1–22, v. 17, 18, 26–42, vi. 9–15, vii. 54, viii. 4,
ix. 1, 2 and xii. 1–4, where Herod acted at the instigation of
the religious authorities—"because he saw it pleased the
Jews."

and courage and sincerity, spread their belief throughout the known world. These same people, seven weeks before their campaign began, had been timid, uncertain, and powerless. This extraordinary and enormously influential change must be accounted for somehow. They themselves accounted for it by saying that their crucified Master had risen from the dead, that they had seen Him alive, and that He had spoken to them, commissioned them and sent them His Spirit to teach and guide and encourage and strengthen them. Now it is perfectly obvious that they themselves sincerely believed this—so sincerely that they not only died for it and suffered torture for it but spent their lives in working for it, amid opposition and difficulties and hardships.

Could it have been a collective hallucination? Apart from the extreme difficulty of believing in a collective—as distinct from an individual —hallucination strong enough to make every person affected by it, live and suffer and die for it, not only together but very often alone: besides this, it must be considered that the disciples were very obviously not expecting anything of the kind. True, Jesus had prophesied it[1]; but on the first occasion Peter had tried to turn Him from going to His death—ignoring apparently the prophecy of the resurrection—while on the second they frankly did not understand Him[2]. So that when Jesus died, they thought that all was

---

[1] Mark viii. 31, ix. 31, x. 34.   [2] Mark viii. 32, ix. 32.

over. The women, immediately after the sabbath brought spices for His embalming. We are even told in the Fourth Gospel that Peter and six other disciples were going back to their old trade of fishing[1]. But suddenly this all changed. They were convinced that they had seen Jesus alive and that He had spoken to them and that not once but several times; that finally they had seen Him ascend from the earth and "a cloud received Him out of their sight." Whereupon angels had prophesied to them of His return[2]. Well, you cannot explain twelve hundred years of history on the hypothesis of an extremely improbable collective hallucination[3]. Whatever the fact may mean, whether the first Christians interpreted it aright or not, the fact itself seems undeniable.

Yet perhaps they were not far wrong when they took the Resurrection as the great proof of the Divinity of Jesus. It certainly seems to set Him apart from other men. We must remember that we are dealing with facts, though with astonishing and unusual ones. And the extraordinarily strong evidence in favour of the Resurrection sheds some light upon the other miraculous events that are alleged to have been connected with Jesus. He is recorded to have healed sick persons, to have performed such natural wonders as walking on the sea and feeding five thousand people with a few

[1] John xxi. 3.   [2] Acts i. 9–11.
[3] Cf. the Rev. W. Temple in *The Faith and Modern Thought*, Lecture III (Macmillan & Co.).

loaves and fishes, and even to have raised the dead. Now again, it is primarily a question of evidence. The evidence it must be confessed is good. The Gospel of St Mark (which is, as we have seen, the oldest of the four and probably the one most directly derived from eye-witnesses) is exceptionally full of records of miracles. The last six chapters are taken up with the last week of the life of Jesus. In the first ten are recorded seventeen distinct miracles [1] besides four [2] occasions on which a number were healed of their diseases at one time. Twelve of these are miracles of healing; and among the diseases healed are "possession by a devil"—i.e. some form of raving madness—and the mysterious disease of leprosy, then considered quite incurable, and still, I believe, without any absolute and certain cure. This class of miracles can of course be explained as "Psychiatry"—but no one has yet fully explained "Psychiatry." Still, Jesus is not the only man who has had a mysterious power of healing. The miracles of nature are more difficult. Four are recorded by St Mark—the calming of a storm [3], walking on the sea [4], and the feeding of the five thousand and of the four thousand [5].

[1] Mark i. 23–26, 30–31, 40–42, ii. 3–12, iii. 1–5, iv. 37–39, v. 2–15, 25–29, 38–42, vi. 35–44, 48–51, vii. 26–30, 32–35, viii. 1–9, 22–25, ix. 17–27, x. 46–52.
[2] Mark i. 32–34, iii. 10, 11, vi. 5, 56.
[3] Mark iv. 37–39.
[4] Mark vi. 48–51.
[5] Mark vi. 35–44, viii. 1–9.

Most difficult of all are the miracles of raising the dead. Three are recorded—of Jairus' daughter[1], of the widow's son at Nain[2], and of Lazarus[3]. The three accounts of the first of these may all well be taken from one source. The second is told simply, almost incidentally, by St Luke alone. The third only occurs in the Fourth Gospel but is told strikingly and circumstantially. Perhaps it is simpler to accept than to reject them, strange as they are. All these miracles can be explained away[4] by coincidence and such things; but these explanations never seem to me to be quite satisfactory. It seems almost easier to believe in the occurrence of these unexplained phenomena in the life of one who is already so strikingly distinguished from His fellow-men, and of whom the Resurrection is recorded, than it is to believe in so strange a series of coincidences. Besides, when each individual miracle is explained away, the total impression made by Jesus, of which these stories are at least the expression, is not, even so, explained. But in any case the miracles are unimportant. Even according to their actual historians they were so regarded by Jesus who tried to hush them up whenever possible[5] and He always re-

---

[1] Matt. ix. 23–26; Mark v. 38–42; Luke viii. 49–56.

[2] Luke vii. 11–15.

[3] John xi. 1–44.

[4] See App. to *The Lord of all Good Life* by Donald Hankey (Longmans & Co.).

[5] Mark i. 44, iii. 12, v. 43, vii. 33, 36, viii. 26 but v. 19 is

fused any demand for a "sign[1]." To say therefore that Christianity stands or falls with the miracles of Jesus is stupidity carried almost to the point of dishonesty.

It is the same with the Virgin Birth. Belief in this doctrine depends very much on one's own definition of the Divinity of Jesus. Perhaps it is not more difficult to believe than the Resurrection —for which as we have seen the evidence is over-whelming; but the evidence for this is not much —a passage in St Matthew's Gospel[2], another in St Luke's[3] but it is not mentioned in St Mark, the Fourth Gospel or the Epistles.

Again, this is not of the essence of Christianity. A man may be the supreme revelation of GOD without being born of a virgin. The uniqueness of Jesus lies, not in such earthly details as these but in His character, His teaching, His life and His death. You may treat them as being on a par with the legends of the saints, you may accept them but try to explain them "naturally," or you

an exception, since Gadara was outside the ordinary scope of His journeys as were also Tyre and Sidon (Mark vii. 24). All the other miracles when Jesus did not command secrecy were either done privately in the presence of His disciples only, or else so publicly that secrecy was impossible. I am only speaking now of those recorded by Mark.

[1] Matt. xvi. 1–4.

[2] Matt. i. 18–25. This passage, moreover, occurs in a section which also contains such stories as the Star, Herod's anxiety about the new king, the visit of the Magi, the flight into Egypt.

[3] Luke i. 34, 35.

may say that if Jesus rose from the dead it is a light matter to believe that He also healed lepers, calmed storms, raised the dead, or was born of a virgin. But it is not worth quarrelling about: the destructive critic may be right or wrong, but he has taken nothing from true Christianity by rejecting them. Jesus is no more to be considered the supreme revelation of GOD on account of His miracles than Socrates is to be regarded as a supreme philosopher because of the manner of his death.

CHAPTER VIII

SIN, PENITENCE, AND ATONEMENT

"WE have left undone those things which we ought to have done and we have done those things which we ought not to have done."

Perhaps that is a good general definition of sin, —that is, of Moral Evil. Sin is evil as it affects our actions: Ugliness, evil as it affects our perceptions: Error, evil as it affects our intellects: and Pain, evil as it affects our bodies. But the English character has in this matter been most unfortunately and deeply tinged by Puritanism, chiefly I suppose, because we are a "practical!" race,— given to doing things, and idolising great doers; rather than aesthetic (or apt to perceive, and to idolise great perceivers), or intellectual (or especially able to think and understand, and likely to idolise great thinkers and understanders). The "ordinary" Englishman is pretty sure, in his rough "practical" way, of the boundary between right and wrong: he cares little for the boundary between true and false: while the boundary between beautiful and ugly he is apt to treat with supreme contempt. He will talk of "a mere aesthete," or "a mere intellectual," but not of "a mere good and honest man"! This is really an utterly false point of view. Evil is evil, and good is good, in any sphere; and who shall say that the sphere of earthly acts is more important than the sphere of intellectual understanding, or of artistic appreciation?

I have called pain physical evil: all parallels are likely to be more or less weak: but it may be useful to try to draw a parallel between pain and sin—between bodily evil and moral evil. The parallel might be extended to cover other forms of spiritual evil, such as error and ugliness: but these for the moment are not our concern.

Pain is the sign that there is something wrong in the body. It may be active disease, or merely a weakness: yet to this extent it is useful and healthy, that it does give warning when something is wrong. It is the protest of a normally healthy organism against ill-health. Besides, without pain there could be no growth—just as no intellect can grow and be enriched without occasional error, and art can never progress without some unsuccessful experiments. But the healthy body tries to rid itself of the cause of its pain, and return to health. Now apply this to sin. Sin[1] is the sign that something is wrong in the soul, or the will—it may be a latent viciousness, or merely weakness; yet it is better that this hidden fault should come to light than remain to fester.

[1] By sin, I mean the outward word or thought as distinguished from the inward moral wrong or weakness which it denotes.

Whiles rank corruption, mining all within,
Infects unseen[1].

If the fault is in the will, it becomes no worse by
an open act. And the true man is striving after
goodness; therefore what we call the conscience
gives a sense of sin, and all that is good in the man
rises against the sin and endeavours to cure the
fault of will. Moreover, sinlessness is not a
practical ideal in this life. This does not mean
that sin does not matter, any more than error and
ugliness do not matter because they are sometimes
inevitable; but our treatment of sin is apt to be
somewhat curious. If a man is in intellectual
error, if he makes an unsuccessful experiment in
art, and then sees his mistake, he doesn't sit down
and cry over spilt milk; what he does, if he is a
man, is to learn from his mistake and set out on a
new path. He recognises where he has failed or
gone wrong and goes ahead along what now seems
the right way. But when a man sins, he is expected to spend a long time in penitence morbidly
confessing his many sins and abasing and hum-
bling himself, till only too often he comes to regard
himself as a creature in whom is no good; his hope
is withered, and at best he begins to aim at sinlessness rather than active goodness, at merely avoiding what is wrong, rather than doing what is right.
This negative goodness is a most insidious and
poisonous ideal.

[1] *Hamlet*, III. iv. 148.

I dreamed I sat by heaven's gate,
    And watched the good men go
All comfortless in robes of white,
    That had no stain to show.

For, fearing greatly, they on earth
    Scarce dared to draw a breath
—Their single talent still unused—
    And now their life was death.

Then I descended to the depth,
    And watched the sinners go,
With faces shining like the day,
    And scarlet robes aglow.

And there among them as of old
    Walked One, Whom I knew well,
Who opened wide His arms to me:
    I found my Christ in hell[1].

Evil, as we have seen, is both negative—weakness or slackness; and positive—a definite vitiation of will. But good is positive. For my own part, give me a sturdy sinner rather than a good man whose only goodness is avoiding sin, who lacks the courage even to be bad, much more to be really good. These are the nonentities whom Dante saw, rejected by heaven and scorned by hell, outcasts even from the pit. Do you think that GOD is to be appeased by whining? "Wherefore criest thou unto Me?...Go forward!" "Don't sit down and cry over spilt milk; recognise your fault; learn from it; strive against it and do better. Set out on a new path; go ahead; do right.

[1] H. Rex Freston, *Collected Poems*, p. 73.

GOD wants servants not slaves." The victorious soldier is not he who avoids defeat by never entering the battle at all. There is more hope for a determined sinner than for a weakling pietist. Sin hinders the soul's perfection, whether negatively or positively: it is an enemy to be fought with, not avoided. Loathing of past sin is the first part of true penitence and an essential part, in so far as it enables you to avoid sin in future. But if a runner falls he does not sit and cry, "How stupid," "How unworthy of me to fall," he gets up and goes on again. The best and truest penitence is to fix your eyes again on the ideal which you had forsaken or denied. Up, and on again! Hope is an essential part of true penitence.

To come to matters more definitely theological. Has the death of Jesus any connection with our sins or help for sinners; and if so, how? The old idea, of course, ran something as follows: God is bound to punish sin. Man sinned: God was therefore bound to punish him, as a sort of debt to the devil, or to His own "justice." So a remedy was found: God became man in Jesus. Jesus did not sin: but He paid the penalty of sin; thus man became free, whoever claimed the wiping-out of sin's debt in Jesus' Blood.

> When before the Judge we tremble,
>   Conscious of His broken laws,
> May the Blood of His atonement
>   Cry aloud, and plead our cause;
> > (Hymn 102, A. & M.).

Or again:

> O sinner, mark, and ponder well
>   Sin's awful condemnation;
> Think what a sacrifice it cost
>   To purchase thy salvation;
> Had Jesus never bled and died,
> Then what could thee and all betide
>   But uttermost damnation?
>
> (Hymn 104, A. & M.).

This theory is logical and businesslike. But there are two things ascribed in it to GOD which seem rather undignified—the discrepancy between His love and His "justice," and the keeping of moral account-books. It has already been hinted that punishment must be remedial, not revengeful. Eternal punishment is not only a confession of failure on the part of GOD—even the extinction of a soul would be that—but it would be a useless and childish piece of revenge as well. Moreover, it could not be even just, for justice, as Plato pointed out[1], can never make a man worse.

Again, morality cannot be run on a system of debit and credit. Nor can vicarious righteousness be counted righteousness at all—a righteousness, so to speak, merely laid on top of a man's imperfections. Righteousness is a quality of the soul. How, then, does the death of Jesus affect man's soul? That it does so is evident; sinners have at all times found comfort and hope in the Cross;

---

[1] *Republic,* Book I. 335 D, E.

this cannot be all false superstition, though probably these penitents themselves could not always, nor perhaps even often have explained exactly how the comfort and hope came to them from the Cross of Jesus—they may only have known that so it was. But take hold of the root principle of Christianity: apply the fundamental principle of Jesus' teaching to Jesus' own life and death. He revealed God as love in His own death, which He suffered for the sake of men because He persisted in His teaching and His opposition to the formalism and hypocrisy that destroyed love. By His death He symbolised and revealed the love of GOD. In Jesus—as in the less conspicuous examples of all others who have shown that love than which no man can have greater, in laying down their lives for their fellow men—in these, men have seen the love of GOD, the supreme ideal, in whose light their sins are most loathsome, in whose beams are hope and strength for the renewed fight, the onward journey.

Those who have felt and realised the love of God revealed in the Cross of Jesus no longer obey the law as a moral code of commands and penalties; they simply cannot offend against such love.

. . . God's dear Son came down to earth and died
In bloodshed and the darkness of clouds that groaned
    aghast
With pierced hands and a great wound in His side.
It is not in my heart to hate the pleasant sins I
    leave.

Earth's passion flames within me fierce and strong.
But this is like a shadow ever rising up to thieve
Sin's pleasures and the lure of every pattern lust can
   weave
And charm of all things that can do him wrong[1].

In Jesus we see GOD'S love and the beauty of
sacrifice. We know GOD better now.

Oh that the heavens were rent and one came down
Who saw men's hurt with kindlier eyes than mine,
Fiercelier than I resented every wrong,
Sweated more painful drops than these that flow
In nightly passion for my people's sin[2],—

and that is what we now have. Our new knowledge of the love of GOD is a far nobler, as well as
a far stronger incentive to hate the evil and follow
the good than the fear of eternal torment, against
which all that loves freedom revolts in scathing
passion, in hatred and scorn and defiance.

Were it not thus, o King of my salvation,
   Many would curse to thee and I for one,
Fling thee thy bliss and snatch at thy damnation,
   Scorn and abhor the shining of the sun,...

Is there not wrong too bitter for atoning?
   What are these desperate and hideous years?
Hast Thou not heard Thy whole creation groaning,
   Sighs of the bondsmen, and a woman's tears[3]?

[1] F. W. Harvey, *Gloucestershire Friends: Poems from a German Prison Camp*, p. 70.

[2] F. W. H. Myers, *St John the Baptist* (*Poems*, p. 64).

[3] F. W. H. Myers, *Saint Paul*.

Or again:

> What! out of senseless Nothing to provoke
> A conscious Something to resent the yoke
>   Of unpermitted Pleasure under pain
> Of Everlasting Penalties, if broke!
>
> What! from his helpless Creature be repaid
> Pure Gold for what he lent us dross-allay'd—
>   Sue for a Debt he never did contract,
> And cannot answer—Oh the sorry trade!
>
> Nay, but, for terror of his wrathful Face
> I swear I will not call Injustice Grace[1].

But the antidote to sin is the Love of GOD.

[1] FitzGerald, *Omar Khayyam*, 2nd ed. st. lxxxiv. to lxxxvi.

CHAPTER IX

MORALITY, TRUTH, AND BEAUTY

THE spiritual activities of mankind may be roughly classified as moral, intellectual and aesthetic. The aim of the first is morality or righteousness; its evil is sin; its physical manifestation is in thoughts and acts. The aim of the second is truth or knowledge; its evil is error; its physical manifestation is in opinions and words. The aim of the third is beauty; its evil is ugliness; its physical manifestation is in art. The perfect man, then, appreciates alike righteousness, truth and beauty. All these paths lead to the same end. The whole perfection of mankind depends on the perfection of each part. Therefore, though total perfection is the ultimate and ideal result of all, each must be an end in itself, and a law to itself.

Now among the English race, the chief difficulty in keeping morality, truth and beauty distinct, is our inherited Puritanical idea of the overwhelming importance of morality. The result is, that seekers after truth and beauty are liable to be interfered with by hide-bound moralists, who do not realise that perfect truth and perfect beauty are bound in the end to be found on the side of morality. Perfection is comprehensive, not exclusive, and principles that seem superficially incompatible are often, if not always, found to be really complementary.

Take the case of Psychical Research. A certain number of men undertook this study in a purely scientific spirit: abuses crept in, charlatans appeared, moral degradation resulted in weak or insincere persons. In comes our "moralist." "Away with it," he cries, too blind or too impatient to distinguish between science and charlatanry, sincerity and hypocrisy, enquiry after truth and greed of money or notoriety. So able and sincere scientists are sometimes pilloried as charlatans; or even as practisers of the black art; their opponents cry out in the name of a spurious morality, or a still more spurious religion, babbling confusedly about "wizards that peep and that mutter." Of whom enough.

Worse and more common is the harm done in the name of morality to art. Now there is no harm for example, in painting a picture with a moral purpose; but do not call that art. Art seeks beauty, and beauty alone. In so far as it succeeds in this it is good; in so far as it fails in this, it is bad. Morality has no place, as such, in art, which is strictly non-moral, just as truth is non-moral. Much in art that seems immoral is not immoral—to the pure all things are pure: if a so-called work of art is really immoral, it is not appealing to the sense of beauty, but to something else—sensuousness, lust or what not.

Righteousness is concerned with earthly acts,

and the motives that prompt them. In these is a vision of GOD the All-Righteous. But no less, to many indeed far more inspiring, is the vision of GOD the TRUTH, revealed in contemplation of truth, of the revelations of truth in the great thinkers and scientists of the world, who have been thus the prophets of GOD—in Plato and Aurelius, Galileo and Newton, James Watt and Frederick Myers. Nor less exalting is the vision of GOD the All-Beautiful, revealed in nature and art, in dawn and sunset, hill and valley, river and ocean; in all music and poetry, painting and sculpture and architecture. What soul that is not, so far as this, dead, can contemplate without a beating exaltation the supreme works of great artists? GOD is revealed in the work of the builders of Wells, the saints of Angelico, the odes of Keats, the figures of Pheidias. And then we imagine GOD as merely the stern Judge, or worse, as the balancer of moral account books, or the capricious but unfortunately omnipotent Despot!

This tyranny of a narrow and unsympathetic morality has sometimes caused a reaction even in England, and men have arisen to decry morality in the interests especially of art. This is of course unsound, and schools of art founded on it are doomed. But it is a significant symptom. Yet were morality discredited, it would be as bad as if art or science was discredited; all man's activities are necessary to his perfection; and all are included and summed up in the grand root principle of Christianity, which is love; and GOD is Love.

CHAPTER X

IMMORTALITY

One dieth in his full strength, being wholly at ease and quiet....

And another dieth in the bitterness of his soul, and never eateth with pleasure.

They shall lie down alike in the dust, and the worms shall cover them. (Job xxi. 23, 25, 26.)

THE question of life after death is one of the most important questions regarding the conduct of our life on earth. If there is no future life, then let us eat and drink, for tomorrow we die.

Drink! for you know not whence you came, nor why: Drink! for you know not why you go, nor where[1].

This, though hopeless, is logical. The pleasures of earth may be low, transitory, unsatisfying, but they are pleasant, and all you have. Enjoy them while you can, and live for the moment. When tired of life, rid yourself of it speedily and painlessly and all is over. But somehow this does not satisfy the soul of man. Man has always had a hankering after continued life, when the instinct has been healthy. Nirvana is only the ideal of a weary and decadent race. Moreover, our very

---

[1] FitzGerald, *Omar Khayyam*, 2nd ed. st. lxxx.

ideals of virtue are only valid in the light of immortality. Is a man good who refrains from wronging his neighbours? But if this life is all, a man who can steal his neighbours' goods without being caught is the happier, and the happiest is he who can do whatever he desires, and yet keep the esteem and praise, and obtain the honours and rewards of his fellow-men. In other words, the happiest man is the successful criminal[1]! The remark that wrongdoing hurts the soul is meaningless, for man has no soul. To say that a criminal is punished by his own conscience merely strengthens the case: for the possession of a conscience argues a certain amount of good in a man; therefore, the worse a man is, the less conscience he will have to trouble him, and the happier he will be. "Ask him, if this life is all, who wins the game?" You may say that a man should serve virtue for no reward: but virtue itself is now only a social agreement—nothing more. As, therefore, we have throughout granted the existence of ideals, and have seen reason to believe in the existence of a supreme and supremely good GOD (who yet certainly does not enforce goodness in this life), we cannot but grant that life is continued beyond bodily death. Modern science is beginning to tell us the same thing.

But "with what body do they come?" Or have they any body at all? Can we in any sense say we believe in the Resurrection of the Body?

[1] Cf. Plato, *Republic*, Book II. 359 B–362 C.

Now obviously this cannot be taken literally. Our present earthly material body lies down in the dust, and the worms cover it: or it is burnt: or it is maimed and scarred. A man is blown to pieces by a shell: will his body, scattered in fragments, become manure for the fruits of the ground?

> When the earth breaks into blossom
> Richer from the dust of man[1],

—shall this rise again?

> Yes! tho' the darts exasperate and bloody
> Fell on the fair side of Sebastian faint,
> Think ye the round wounds and the gashes ruddy
> Scar in God's house the beauty of the saint?[2]

Literal interpretation, then, being impossible, the thin end of the wedge is in. Speculation is more free. Perhaps the soul will form itself a body adapted to its new surroundings, whatever they may be—a body, perhaps, like that which St Paul describes[3], related to our earthly body in the same sort of way as a flower or tree is related to its seed. Or perhaps the soul will need no body—that is no material expression. But this at least it must mean, and this at least we must grant: that the personality of a man continues after his death, that he takes his character with him—for his character is his soul. And as earthly life is social,

[1] *Outward Bound*, by an officer who has since fallen in Gallipoli (*The Times*, 27 Aug. 1915).

[2] F. W. H. Myers, *Final Perseverance* (*Poems*, p. 71).

[3] 1 Cor. xv. 35–44.

so must be our next life, and friends shall recognise each other somehow.

Human imagination has always played round the details of our next life. This is very natural, but no detailed description can be entirely satisfactory. But one point has brought forth some very queer theories: the tormenting question, What of those who die "in sin"—to use a theological term? This cuts two ways: a man usually regards his enemies as sinful, but he cannot always be quite satisfied about the "fitness to die"—to use another horrible phrase—even of those whom he loves. But the first usually predominates. The great influence on European thought in this matter has been the dreams of the post-exilic Jewish Apocalyptic writers; who, belonging to an oppressed and proud and passionate nation, imagined and prophesied terrible things in store for their powerful and victorious enemies. Accordingly, eternal punishment became early, and for a long time remained, a prominent tenet of the Church. The objections to this have already been briefly noted: it is inconsistent with even man's love, justice, or common sense: much more with GOD's. A compromise has been suggested—the theory of Annihilation, or Conditional Immortality—that if a soul persists in evil, it eventually rots out of existence. This theory is open to some of the same objections. GOD first creates a soul and then destroys it. The net result for the soul is this: it awakes to a universe thus governed; it sets itself against, or finds itself incompatible with, this universe. Eventually after much trouble, it returns to the non-existence which it had better never have left, after having first won a partial victory over a universe which produced, but could neither absorb nor coerce it. Thus the soul has suffered much to no purpose, and GOD has in this one instance at least failed. The total result is utter evil.

We seem then to be driven back on Universalism—the theory that at last every single soul must become perfect, or, since perfection is necessarily an infinite process, set itself towards perfection, and cease from its opposition or indifference to good. Up jumps our moralist: "What reason," he demands, "is there any more for men to be good, if all are at last to become perfect and to be saved? If you are sure of your final safety, eat and drink and satisfy your lust. You are undermining the very basis of morality with your sentimental notions." True: I was once told of a girl who after hearing Universalism preached, came to her mother and said that she felt that the prop of her morality had been taken away, and she should fall. And she did fall. But her morality was only propped on fear—fear of punishment: her soul was weak and low: she would probably have fallen in any case sooner or later; and even if not, such morality as hers is more contemptible than the violence of a courageous sinner. But there must be eternal hope; GOD

cannot love her less than her mother did; and
"GOD has plenty of time to do things between now
and the other side of eternity."

But to our moralist's other objection we may
reply that the good and the bad soul cannot be in
the same position. Evil hurts the soul; perfection
is of the soul. Every evil admitted into a soul re-
moves it further from perfection and makes its
future struggle harder, and its gaze on perfection
dimmer. Yet that light can never quite fade. But
a soul rotted by immorality, indifference to truth,
contempt of beauty, or any other evil, is worse
equipped, and finds its goal dimmer and its
struggle harder than a soul strengthened by the
contemplation and pursuit of what is good in act,
true in thought, and beautiful in art. You may
call this remedial punishment if you like—struggle
will make a weak soul stronger—but punishment
for sheer revenge is useless and childish, whether
in man or GOD and unthinkable in perfect Goodness.

There is, then, further progress in the life after
death; and progress means struggle, and perhaps
pain. Perhaps this progress will be endless, since
the goal is infinite; but the idea that all eternity
depends on this little space of earthly life is too
disproportionate to be believed, and too terrible
to be borne. The next life must be a continuation
of this, another stage of the same journey, another
phase of the same battle, not the journey's end, or
the battle's completion.

O nights how desolate, O days how few,
  O death in life, if life be this, be this!
  O weighed alone as one shall win or miss
The faint eternity which shines there thro'!
  Lo all that age is as a speck of sand
Lost on the long beach when the tides are free,
  And no man metes it in his hollow hand
Nor cares to ponder it, how small it be;
  At ebb it lies forgotten on the land
And at full tide forgotten in the sea[1].

And in eternal progress is eternal hope; yes, in regress still is hope. While there is life there is hope; but a "dead soul"—a soul imprisoned and fixed for ever in its evil—there is no hope there; yet neither is there any justice or love or wisdom there. Therefore it cannot be the act of GOD. I could not worship a GOD whom I believe capable of so monstrously evil a thing. All we who have come from GOD shall return to GOD: for if GOD be GOD, Whose power is equal to His Will, no evil will, human or demoniac, shall in the end withstand Him, "that GOD may be all in all."

[1] F. W. H. Myers, *Fragments of prose and poetry*, 1904, p. 172.

CHAPTER XI

CHRISTIANITY

IT may seem that by this time we have worn Christianity rather thin. If it is not necessary to define very strictly the Divinity of Jesus: if the Church is so largely a human institution, its doctrines not infallible, its organisation not determined: if Universalism has excluded from our belief the Last Judgment as an historical event: if the forgiveness of sins is merely perpetual inspiration to do better in the future: what then is left of Christianity as it has been understood in the past? Is it not true that we have merely tried to evolve a theistic and idealistic philosophy and called it Christianity? I say, most emphatically No: we have left the core of Christianity unhidden, its central light unveiled—the principles of Jesus' teaching, His Person, His life, His death. Jesus was the centre of the Apostles' teaching as He has been of all true Christian teaching ever since. The first Christian sermon began with the name of "Jesus of Nazareth[1]," and it is with Him that all right Christianity begins. And thus we are still Christians: yes, and more Christian than those who quarrel about "Faith and Order"—that is

---

[1] Acts ii. 22.

about dogma and organisation. For we try to go back through these to Jesus.

Christianity is an ideal; but in this point it surpasses all other idealistic philosophies and religions—that it is an ideal expressed and summarised in a Person. It is quite literally the religion of the "Word made Flesh"—the Eternal and Absolute expressed as far as may be in human terms. And this Word is Love. In this immense mystic word is inherent the whole good. "Every one that loveth is born of GOD and knoweth GOD. He that loveth not, knoweth not GOD[1]." And one of the most characteristic acts and expressions of love is self-sacrifice. And here lies the unfathomable significance of the Cross.

Not in soft speech is told the earthly story,
     Love of all Loves! that showed thee for an hour:
Shame was thy kingdom, and reproach thy glory,
     Death thy eternity, the Cross thy power[2].

This disposes of the objection that the doctrine of love is a weak and sentimental thing, out of touch with the stern and hard facts of life.

God's love's...
          ...caress IS chastisement.
What answered through the olive-trees
GOD, when the Son in anguish lay,
Praying, "O take this cup away!"
Did He then take it? Nay, child, nay:
He made Him drink it to the lees[3].

[1] I John iv. 7, 8.   [2] F. W. H. Myers, *Saint Paul.*
[3] Ibsen's *Brand*, transl. C. H. Herford, p. 86.

This willing abandonment of self is the highest and noblest and truest love.

"Greater love hath no man than this, that a man lay down his life for his friends," said Jesus; and at another time, "No man taketh it from me, but I lay it down of myself[1]."

> It is not martyrdom to toss
> In anguish on the deadly cross:
> But to have WILL'D to perish so,
> To WILL it through each bodily throe,
> To will it with still-tortured mind,
> This, only this, redeems mankind[2].

In this great principle of love, in one manifestation or another, in the form of sacrifice, harmony, or whatever it may be, is the key and solution of everything. But again, objections may be raised: for example, Are we to love evil? Evil in the abstract is of course hateful and to be hated; as by Dante,

> Who loved well because he hated,
> Hated wickedness that hinders loving[3].

But Dante, in his great poem, could not separate evil from the workers of evil; his hell for evil had to be filled with evil-doers, human types of sin.

---

[1] John xv. 13 and x. 18. These are quoted from the Fourth Gospel. But at the least they are a very ancient commentary of Jesus, by one who had studied His Person and work very deeply, whether the Apostle himself or a disciple of his.

[2] Ibsen's *Brand*, transl. C. H. Herford, p. 92.

[3] R. Browning, *Men and Women. One Word more*, vol. v. p. 315.

But it is a platitude that Christianity hates the sin but loves the sinner. There is a good example of this in the story (whether authentic or not) of Jesus' treatment of the woman taken in adultery. Even if the actual incident is fabulous, the moral importance of the story is not impaired. The Pharisees discovered, at the Feast of Tabernacles, a woman in the very act of adultery. They seized her, and dragged her into the Temple to Jesus, through the middle of the crowd, not by reason of moral disapprobation of the deed—they would not consult Jesus about that—but "that they might have to accuse Him." Now Jesus did not condone the sin; He said she had sinned, but His sentence was not "I condemn thee," nor even, "Go and weep and do penance," it was, "I do not condemn thee; go, and sin no more." At the same time He rebuked the Pharisees for their eagerness to "down" the woman—a type of eagerness not remarkably absent in some who profess and call themselves Christians.

What about our charities for the "deserving poor"? I wonder what Mary Magdalene would have got out of them. Look within; consider your own faults, and you will be less ready to condemn your neighbour. "He that is without sin among you, let him first cast a stone at her." Jesus always proclaimed that His mission was primarily to sinners. "Go ye," He said to the moralists, "and learn what that meaneth, I will have mercy, and not sacrifice; for I am not come to call the righteous, but sinners to repentance." Yet no one can ever say that Jesus took sin lightly. He loathed sin. Though His scale of moral values was utterly different from that of the Pharisees, He was always fighting sin, both in others and in His own temptations. So He laid down the principle that the sinner must be distinguished from the sin, and He put it in practice Himself. This practice has been misunderstood by those who have failed to grasp the principle. Still confusing the sinner and the sin, they have read such stories as that of Jesus' treatment of the wicked woman in the Pharisees' house[1], and have almost seemed to draw the conclusion that He in some way condoned the sin. As a matter of fact He was absolutely silent about the woman's wrong-doings. The secret of the essential distinction lies again in the fundamental principle of love. As in the case of the woman taken in adultery, He concentrated His attention, not on the case, but on the person. This story in St Luke vii. is one of the most beautiful and touching stories in the world; it is so absolutely human. Jesus and the woman were two human beings, met face to face; she loved Jesus, and He loved her. This Pharisee was not human, and he was therefore rebuked and silenced. "Her sins, which are many, are forgiven; for she loved much. ...And He said unto her, Thy sins are forgiven."

And so with Zacchaeus[2]! He repented of his sins: he offered restitution: for he loved Jesus.

[1] Luke vii. 36–50. [2] Luke xix. 1–10.

The Puritans muttered, "He is gone to be the guest of a sinner!" We can imagine them holding up their hands in pious horror. But Jesus preferred a loving and repentant sinner to a loveless "righteous man that needs no repentance." This is strongly brought out in the parable of the Prodigal Son[1]. This young man spends his fortune in riotous and probably immoral living and is reduced to beggary. He goes home in penitence, and his father gives him a royal welcome. His elder brother hears of it, and refuses to come in. "This fellow—he has devoured your living with harlots! *I* never disobeyed you"—yes; but that is not the point. Lovelessness is worse than all other sins[2]. By his behaviour now this elder brother showed that he lacked love, and all this obedience went for nothing in comparison with the penitent love of his sinful brother. The principle is this: Love the sinner, and your loathing of his sin will not cause you to feel contempt or lack of sympathy for him. There is nothing, I think, in the New Testament afterwards like this unique tenderness of Jesus—yet a tenderness not incompatible with hatred of sin[3]. Jesus is the bitter enemy of all sin; but He is also the enemy of any self-righteous Pharisaism. He was very fond of associating with people who were not "respect-

[1] Luke xv. 11–32.
[2] Matt. xxi. 31.
[3] All this is personal, and bears only indirectly on the theory of punishment, which is largely a social question.

able." It was the respectable folk who aroused, by their self-satisfaction and lovelessness, His contempt and anger. Christianity hates sin but loves the sinner.

> Yes, spurned and fool and sinner stray
> Along the highway and the way...
> This journey soon will make them clean:
> Their faith is greater than their sin[1].

Or there is the old objection, If GOD is love, why is there so much evil in the world? There is a story of a preacher who took for the text of his first sermon, "GOD is love." As he gave it out, all the untold evil of the world seemed to flash across his mind, and he silently registered a vow that he would never preach again till he had seen how this could be reconciled with GOD's love. And the story goes that he never did preach again. Yet it is a shallow view that GOD cannot be loving while evil is so rife, or that love cannot be the root principle of so unkind a universe   In reply to this view it may be asked, How is it that, when the world contains so much evil, men have ever come to regard GOD as loving? It is not merely the sentimentality of unsound idealists; the view has been held by men of practical and personal experience of the world's evil, men too of sound, hard, worldly wisdom, who have met evil of all kinds, and still continue to call GOD Love.

Moreover, such a view is very largely unfair to

[1] C. H. Sorley, *Marlborough and other poems* (3rd edn), p. 107.

GOD. Take this present War. It has come as a grand text to those who want to disprove GOD's benevolence or His existence. "Look at this," they say, "the barbarities, the horrors, the pain and the waste and death, the slaughter of innocents, the torture of those who did no harm, the death of so many who might have done much for the world. Consider these facts, and say, if you dare, that GOD, if He exists at all, is love!" But was it GOD after all, that caused this War? Or was it man? Can you put down to GOD the national jealousies and rivalries and suspicions and greedinesses that were the seed that has burst into this poisonous and flaming flower of death? You serve evil, you love yourself, you strive against your neighbour, and when you find that you have brought disaster on yourself, you blame GOD for it! You ask for trouble, and when you get it you cry out on GOD. Of course, certain people will point out with righteous indignation, that *we* are not responsible for this War, *our* hands are clean, *we* were a peaceful people, meekly inheriting the earth, till that monster of Satan, Germany, brutally and inexcusably attacked us. Well; if that is your view, be it so. Say the evil is all of German make. It is still evil. The problem has changed, and become, "Why if GOD is loving and just does He allow the innocent to suffer for the sins of the guilty?" For such is most undoubtedly the case on the earth. We are compelled to fall back on our principle of love. The whole human race—including the Germans—are one, and one member must suffer with and for another. It is inevitable. "What?" you say, "are we to love the Germans?" We must at any rate recognise that the Germans are men, as we are men. Men at the Front, who tend German wounded, and feed starving German prisoners, know this; the excess of hatred seems to be a luxury chiefly enjoyed at home. This recognition of kinship, however, does not preclude killing the enemy, if, as now, it is necessary. The view that it does, assumes that death is necessarily an evil and killing necessarily wrong. It may be impossible—as it is now—to stamp out the evil without killing the evil-doer; yes, and without killing those, too, whom we believe to be doing the work of evil, but who think themselves to be doing good, and who are as innocent of actually causing the War as we are. Killing may be a necessity, though an unfortunate one—the lesser of two evils. This argument, I know, will not appeal to "plain minds" incapable of separating in their thought even things absolutely distinct. But there it is.

The ultimate problem is really this: Why does GOD allow evil at all, if He really is loving? It is these objectors who take a sentimental view of love rather than we. Their idea of love is the foolish love of a mother who spoils her child. A wiser and nobler and stronger love is that which desires the loved ones' highest good; and if this cannot be obtained without pain—well then, pain be it

"His caress is chastisement." But it may still be wondered why we are not allowed an Adam-and-Eve existence in a calm, untroubled and sinless garden, a land of unvexed peace and unmingled pleasure,

> Where falls not hail, or rain, or any snow,
> Nor ever wind blows loudly; but it lies
> Deep-meadow'd, happy, fair with orchard-lawns,
> And bowery hollows crown'd with summer sea[1].

But this is most ignoble wonder. Which is better, the innocence of a child, or the goodness of a good man? The one is merely good because he cannot be anything else, the other is good, because he loves good, and his goodness is stronger through the falls he has tried with evil. GOD'S plan

> Was to create man and then leave him,
> Able, His own word saith, to grieve Him,
> But able to glorify Him too,
> As a mere machine could never do...
> Made perfect as a thing of course[2].

Without the possibility of evil there could be no good; without freewill there could be no virtue. Man's highest good could not possibly be attained without the strengthening and purifying power of contest; he could not even know what good was had he not seen and known evil. Therefore the love of GOD which desires our highest good, has decreed that we shall know good and evil and

---

[1] Tennyson, *Morte d'Arthur*.
[2] Browning, *Christmas Eve and Easter Day*.

shall have the choice between them, which shall be ours.

This may be thought inconsistent with the notion that in the long run every one shall become perfect. No; for now we are dealing with eternity. If the love of GOD has decreed that man's good shall be made good in battle, it has also decreed that none shall be finally lost in that battle; yet those who are weak or cowardly or treacherous cannot but pay the penalty. It rests with the man's own soul what he shall suffer before he conquers. We cannot conceive to what extremities the love of GOD may have to go before a man will see that good is his good and so take sides against evil.

Love, then, is the key of the universe, its heart, its foundation-stone. Love is the source and the end of morality, the supreme truth, and the ideal beauty. In morality, for example, there seems superficially to be two opposing principles—law and liberty. The latter is usually regarded as the negation of morality, a revolt against the moral law of "Thou shalt not" or "Thou shalt." The law says, "Thou shalt not commit adultery," or positively, "Thou shalt keep thy body in temperance." The law-abider refrains from adultery and keeps his body in temperance: the libertine commits it, and yields to his body. That is the usual contrast. But what really is liberty? Take an extreme definition: it is doing what one likes. Now suppose a man likes temperance and hates adultery

—does he not then keep the law in doing what he likes? This law is not then irksome to such a man. In other words, law and liberty are united in one in Love. And even the law itself is thus strengthened, for the man who loves the law keeps its spirit as well as its letter. Love is the highest law, and the truest liberty. Morality is not a matter of good or bad acts, but of good or bad motives. The difference between a righteous man and an unrighteous is not in their open acts, but in their wills. A man who does wrong believing it to be right is more righteous than a man who does right for a selfish or otherwise low motive. Take the example of a rich man who founds a hospital or an almshouse. All applaud him; but does he do it out of pity and love for the sick and poor, or does he do it to win the praise of men, and perhaps their honours— for laudatory notices in the papers, and perhaps a knighthood? It is on this question that the merit of the deed depends. He has obeyed the letter of the law that a man must help his fellow-men, and especially those who are "worse off" than himself; but if his motive is low he may or he may not get his earthly reward—he is certainly no real gainer. He is none the better for his act, even though the poor may be happier for it and bless him for it. Love is the moral law; and if his will loves good he is righteous; but though he bestows all his goods to feed the poor and have not love, it profiteth him nothing. Though he speak with the tongues of men and of angels, though he understand all things hidden, and have all knowledge and all faith, though he yield up even his body to be burnt, and have not love, he is nothing. Righteous acts done without love are nothing. A cup of cold water given in the name of love is all —it has struck the root of the matter, the very core and centre of all morality.

Nor is love less essential and central in the intellectual sphere. What is Truth? Ask the scientist what is the supreme and guiding principle of the sphere of his study; it is order, he will say. And what is order in human terms, but love? What ordered state was ever securely based on anything but love? "Alexander, Caesar, Charlemagne, and myself," said Napoleon, "founded Empires on force and they are gone; Jesus Christ alone founded His on love, and to-day millions would die for Him." A perfectly ordered state, if such ever existed, would be a state where (as Plato says) every one does his own work—the work he is suited for; the most richly endowed would do the highest and hardest work, the less richly endowed would do inferior work; but all the jealousies, all undue ambitions, would be prevented by the love of each man for the state and for his fellow-citizens. Love is thus the source of order and humility.

Or ask the Philosopher. We have heard what Plato says; let us next hear Aurelius. "We are made for co-operation, like feet, like hands, like eye-lids, like rows of the upper and lower teeth.

To act against one another then is contrary to nature[1]." "The good for the reasonable animal is society[2]." "Reverence the gods and help men[3]." "Love mankind[4]." "Men exist for the sake of one another[5]."

Order is in the stars above; order is virtue in the sight of the reason that seeks truth; order is the virtue of mankind as a social being; and order means love. The inferior must be inferior; but where love rules, order is firm; for selfishness is quelled. Harmony and due subordination, sacrifice and love, are supreme Truth.

And this love must be applied to matters of dogma and religious organisation; unity of spirit may and must be present, even though uniformity of organisation is impossible. But when a bishop of the Church of Christ is found rejecting fellow-Christians from the great Christian Sacrament of the Lord's Supper because the organisation of their body is not the same as his, or excommunicating a fellow bishop for favouring a man darkly suspected of "heresy"—that is, of freely exercising his individual reason on matters of theology —or when another bishop is found loudly protesting against a fellow priest's appointment to the Episcopate on similar grounds—then the enemies of the Lord blaspheme, and what are we Christians to say? At the time of the Kikuyu contro-

[1] *Meditations*, II. 1.   [2] *Ibid*. V. 16.
[3] *Ibid*. VI. 30.   [4] *Ibid*. VII. 31.
[5] *Ibid*. VIII. 59.

versy, when "fellow-Christians" were bitterly abusing each other over the Sacrament of love, a cartoon appeared—I forget where—entitled "Saving the Heathen," and showing an African savage grinning while he watched one Christian "bishop" hitting another over the head—in the name of Christ,

> Whose sad face on the Cross sees only this
> After the passion of a thousand years[1].

This sort of thing is a disgrace to Christianity; "for in Jesus Christ neither circumcision availeth any thing nor uncircumcision; but faith which worketh by love[2]." Love is the highest truth— love and sacrifice and harmony.

Or what of the aesthetic faculty, the desire and search for beauty? Love is the supremely beautiful thing. That sublimest example of love, the death of Jesus, has been one of the greatest inspirations of art, from the calm grandeur of the crowned Christ of Byzantine art, and the serene splendour of Fra Angelico in San Marco at Florence, to the passionate loneliness of Guido Reni's interpretation in San Lorenzo at Rome. The spell of beauty is very near akin to love—is indeed love. It is love that is awakened by the sight of rolling hills and rich valleys, of the quiet stars, of some grand cathedral, or some superb picture, by some perfect ode or some sublime

[1] R. Browning, *Fra Lippo Lippi*, vol. v. p. 239.
[2] Gal. v. 6.

sonata. Oscar Wilde was moved by the supreme aesthetic beauty of the life of Jesus. The incidents of Jesus' life and death have been the subject of a thousand magnificent achievements in all branches of art. Love is again the supreme beauty and inspiration of beauty.

Religion is the quintessence of human activities. Nothing that is truly human is alien to it. All human enjoyment, all right laughter, is of the nature of religion. There seems to be a popular notion that religion is something very serious, something arcane, hidden and shielded from healthy human life. It is not. He who prays attends to religion; he who engages in honest trade attends to religion; so does he who studies science or practises' art; so does he who laughs. A hearty laugh sounds the praise of GOD. Religion was not only the source of the Greek tragic and comic drama: it was the source of our English dance and drama. The "Mystery Plays" were religious dramas, representing scenes from the life of Jesus or the saints; they were also comic—often coarse according to our modern ideas. Religion is a happy thing. It is again the Puritans who must bear most of the blame for our forgetting this. They had, unfortunately, no sense of humour. GOD, I believe, has. Consequently, the Puritans maimed and devitalised religion to a large extent. If we would bring to bear on ecclesiastical and theological matters the same free common sense, the same healthy sense of humour, that we use in other concerns, there would be less bitterness, less schism, less narrowness, less stupidity in our religion. Two men are both seeking GOD, striving after perfection; yet they stand and revile and spit at each other, because they differ, not about GOD, but about Bishops; not about ideals, but about phrases; and so they "hiss and hate." And the blind fight the blind. Common sense would kick these quibbles out of doors. Humour would blow them away in a storm of laughter. We want more of this free and healthy humour in these matters. At present we acknowledge Zeus and Apollo and Prometheus and Athena—power and light and sacrifice and wisdom—in the Godhead; but we have forgotten Pan and Dionysus—the spirit of bursting nature and of jolly enjoyment.

All things properly human are religious. Everything good is religious, everything that is not evil. And the criterion of good and evil is to be found in Jesus' principle of love. Everything which does not offend against love is good. But in this world evil is strong; and we have no reason to believe that immediately after death things will be much easier. Progress must be by struggle and pain. The Christian call is not a sentimental lullaby of ease; it is a call to strength and manhood, a summons to do and suffer, to strive and endure,

> ...eternally to DO—
> Our joy, our task, our recompense;
> Up unexploréd mountains move,
> Track tireless through great wastes afar,

Nor slumber in the arms of love,
Nor tremble on the brink of war;
Make Beauty and make Rest give place,
Mock Prudence loud—and she is gone,
Smite Satisfaction on the face
And tread the ghost of Ease upon[1].

Christianity is a great and eternal adventure.
Jesus' call was not a call to cowards! "Whosoever
will come after Me, let him deny himself, and take
up his cross, and follow Me." "He that loveth
father or mother more than Me is not worthy of
Me....And he that taketh not his cross, and followeth
after Me, is not worthy of Me. He that findeth his
life shall lose it: and he that loseth his life for My
sake shall find it[2]."

What better wouldst thou have when all is done?
If any now were bidden rise and come
To either, could he pause to choose between
The rose-warm kisses of a waiting bride
In a shut silken chamber, and the thrill
Of the bared limbs bound fast for martyrdom?[3]

Love must be prepared to meet the hate of evil,
yes, even of the men whom it loves, and be able to
love them while it fights to the death against the
evil that is in them. Love cannot conquer without
strength, without endurance. But a man who was
perfectly loving would be perfectly good; he would
also be perfectly free, for he would never desire to

[1] C. H. Sorley, *Marlborough and other poems* (3rd edn),
p. 71.
[2] Mark viii. 34; Matt. x. 37–39.
[3] Mrs Hamilton King, *The Disciples*.

do or think what was evil. He would also have attained supreme Truth and Beauty and the very perfection of humanity. That is our standard, which must be applied to every department of life; and this is the root Christian principle and its supreme ideal, expressed to us in the Word made flesh, the perfectly loving life of Jesus of Nazareth. His teaching laid down the great central principle: His life expressed it in action: and all is summed up in the terrible and wonderful and supreme symbol of His Cross. The seed and full flower of all human goodness is the life and death and love of Jesus.

Finished January 20th, 1918.
Revised July, 1918.

For EU product safety concerns, contact us at Calle de José Abascal, 56–1°,
28003 Madrid, Spain or eugpsr@cambridge.org.

www.ingramcontent.com/pod-product-compliance
Ingram Content Group UK Ltd.
Pitfield, Milton Keynes, MK11 3LW, UK
UKHW012333130625
459647UK00009B/266